MW00911421

You Want to Stop Sinning…Stop

By a Witness, May Lewis

You Want to Stop Sinning…Stop

Editor: LaBrenda Hill

Citations: Thomas Nelson, Inc. (1990). Holy Bible (King James Version). United States of America

"All scriptures are from the book and version stated above unless otherwise indicated."

Copyright © 2018 by May Lewis

All Rights Reserved. This book may not be reproduced in whole or in part, by any means now known or yet to be invented, without the express written permission of the Copyright Owner, excepting brief quotes used in reviews or scholarly journals. The purchase of a copy of this book does not confer upon the purchaser license to use this work or any part therein in other works, including derivatives.

First Printing: 2019
ISBN #: 978-0-359-91379-4
MAY LEWIS
Memphis, TN 38125
USA

2

Dedication

As always, this book and any of the other books that I have written is first dedicated to God the Father and Jesus His Son. It was written to give God the glory and the praise while in the process of feeding His sheep. My next dedication must definitely go to the book of the Bible, being a big inspiration for me in wanting to help others to know God as I do.

In addition, I have to give a special dedication to my entire family whom I love dearly. With that being notated, I would also like to dedicate this book to all of the families of the world. My hope in life is for everyone to be as one big happy family, and to love one another unconditionally as God loves us.

This book was written to encourage all to stop sinning and to stop giving excuses why we cannot stop sinning. Yes, of course, you are right. We have all sinned and no one can throw the first stone. It also means we are all no better than the next person; but it does not mean we cannot stop sinning. That is why the word, "sinned" is written with the suffix "ed" on end. It is in past tense meaning that it should be bygone or in the process of not existing. In addition, since it is written in past tense this should give us hope that we can stop it. God has given us plenty of opportunities to discontinue our actions. The great news is that God wants us all to have eternal life in spite of what we have done or the sin we have committed. The big question is, do we want eternal life?

TABLE OF CONTENTS

FOREWORD

We often say that we can do many things. Some of us even say that we can do two things at the same time. While others may even go a little further and say, they can do five things at once. Of course, do not let us really start bragging. We could say that we are capable of doing 25 or more things single-handed without blinking an eye. Yet, when it is all said and done and the truth is really told, we cannot do ten things that God requested us to do. Do you need a hint of what those are? Nah, I don't think so! You guessed it; it is obeying His Ten Commandments.

We need to stop going around in circles doing the same evil deeds as the Israelites did in the wilderness. As well as, we need to stop acting like the Gentiles, who did whatever that came to their minds. *"For the time past of our life may suffice us to have wrought the will of the Gentiles, when we walked in lasciviousness, lusts, excess of wine, revellings, banquetings, and abominable idolatries" (1 Peter 4:3 King James Version):* We continue doing the same repeated sinful acts by doing things our way. Let me take a moment to simplify it a little bit for you. We need to stop doing whatever we want to do just because it feels good to us; not caring that it is not pleasing to God, or that it might be hurting others. We have to start right now and wake up because what we are really doing is shortening our days here on earth.

Even though sinning can be habit forming, it can also be broken. Just because there is a lot of evilness that surrounds us, we do not have to be a contributor to it. We do though have to want to make a change. This is what makes this particular book so special. This book urges us to take a good deep look at ourselves. It assists us in not being too quick to point fingers at others, and to start immediately our new journey of stop sinning.

You Want to Stop Sinning...Stop

The majority of us are already familiar with the Ten Commandments being mentioned in the Bible in the Old Testament. Yet, some of these same individuals think that the Commandments are now outdated and were not mentioned in the New Testaments. Others believing that in this day and time we only have to obey a few of them.

God gave us some agreements and laws to follow. The Bible informs us of what will happen if we obey the agreements and laws and what will happen if we do not. God wants us to stop our evil ways immediately. Of course, there will still be consequences from being defiant. But at least by stopping, we would have stopped sin in its tracks and been obedient to God. In the long run, it would have a trickle down effect in our family; to our children, grandchildren, and great-grandchildren which would not only extend our days here on this earth, but theirs as well.

Some of our main duties while we are here on this earth are to appreciate God, and be obedient to His laws and agreements. This is the rationale behind this book. Therefore, you can go ahead and hug this book tightly, right here and now because I am going to give you one of the best rundowns of why we should put the brakes on sinning and how.

Chapter 1

ONLY "1" GOD

When you were kids, you may have been given the impression that mom was the "Mother" of all gods. She ensured that you were feed. She even put clothes on our backs. It appeared that when you physically looked around she was the only one you saw standing. No, she was not a god! Yes, mom was the one that had us, but God was the one that created us. There is a lot to thank God for because He is the one that provided the clothes, the food, our health, and do I need to say more? We have to give God all the praises, and serve Him only. There is only but one true God. If we do not, then we could easily get the misperception of putting someone or something in position for God. God commanded us to have no one or nothing that comes before Him. *"No man can serve two masters; for either he will hate the one, and love the other; or else he will hold to the one, and despise the other. Ye cannot serve God and mammon" (Matthew 6:24).* Therefore, we need to stop doing it. Yes, that means not even our friends, money, family members, situations, homes, ourselves, sports, problems, cell phones, sexual activities, illness, cars, our past, etc. should be glorified before God. Yes, this includes the sun, moon, and stars too which some try to magnify and worship instead of God. All our trust should be in God.

Jesus oftentimes reiterated in the Bible that we all have the same one and only Father and God including Himself. Jesus also emphasized to Satan that there was only one true God when Satan tried to tempt Him. Jesus also exemplified in His lifestyle that we should be all about God's business; and not giving into our own selfish desire by doing what we want to do, or mimic the evil we have seen others do.

You Want to Stop Sinning…Stop

When God brought the Israelites out of Egypt, He not only gave the Israelites great cities to live in, but He also gave them Commandments to obey. If they complied, God would not only give them longevity, but they would also be successful in whatever they put their hands on.

God wants to be placed first in our lives and the only one that we come running to when we have an issue. He wants us to tell Him all about our situation first instead of broadcasting to everyone else about our problems. Telling everyone else really only rehashes the situation. It only makes you more angry about the issue when you re-talk about it. Why don't you let God assist you with easing your burden? Others are only a sounding board and make the situation worst as if making a fire more flammable. Believe me, I use to do the same thing too, then I started talking to God first rather than talking to others first.

The first Commandment is so important because it puts God first above all others. We have to show our gratitude for all that God has done for us. My grandmother knew the importance of giving God the praise. She often commented to us, "I am going to put the fear of God in you." This statement let us know first-hand that our grandmother and God was not a joke and neither to be played with. We had to give respect to God and put Him first above all. We came to realize that He knows everything. We could not hide anything from Him. We should always be loyal and love the only one true God with every being in our body. This means that our whole heart should be all into it and there should nothing be left on the table. We should give God no reason to believe that another so-called god has been substituted for Him.

I had decided to stop given God my odds and of course, my ends too. Instead I wanted to do something special since God has been so good to me. I knew that I could never ever pay Him back for all the things He had done. However, I wanted to do something that came from deep down inside my heart. I made a decision to start making a daily sacrifice to God. Of course, it was not relating to animals, but something of more importance. Yes, absolutely, a sacrifice can still be made to God, but in a different fashion. For example: you may refrain from doing something, do something differently, give more time for something and/or someone, give something special to someone else, etc. as long as it all pertains to reverence to God.

Let me go and expound a little bit more of where I am headed. The sacrifice(s) need to be voluntarily of your own free will. In addition, it must be meaningful because you are giving this up or you stop doing something for God. It is a spiritual agreement between you and God. It needs to be something that you are totally engaged in. This daily sacrifice to God can also be related to your time, your heart, mind, or even the way you act, etc.

God is placed, the majority of time, second in our lives. We have a tendency of being selfish and thinking only about ourselves. This is especially why God should be given more of your time. Time is important. There is one thing unique about time, once you've used it or do not decide to use it there is no refund and you cannot get it back. Therefore, we have to make sure that we make good use of it. That is what I started doing.

I had to realize, giving my time was just as important as giving my tithe. I was spending my time during the day the way that I wanted to, with no regards to the Originator that had made me. I was not giving back some of my time which God had given me. Furthermore, when I did decide to give my time, I was giving God only the time out of the day that was leftover. The majority of that time, I was tired and sleepy. Oftentimes, we do make a habit of giving God our time after we had a hard day's work and have no energy left. We then give God a rushed prayer at night right before going to bed, and then say "Amen" as if we just had done God a favor.

Money and possessions have become lesser and lesser or maybe even scarcer in some cases. If you think about it, what is the best thing you can give God besides your funds when trying to give God your all? It's your time. God wants the first fruit of all things, which includes a percentage of your time.

__My Sacrifice:__ *I decided to forget about what I wish to do and make "God" first with the use of my time, and stop wasting it and giving into my own desires. God was going to be first in every aspect of my life before anything, anyone, including myself. God has been blessing me every day with a new beginning of life here on earth. I thought what could be better than the first fruits of my time; and the most important part of the day that He gives me is when I wake up in the morning. Do I need to say any more, time is priceless?*

I started meditating more on His Word. My meditation was first begun by praying and thanking God for waking me up and giving me a new day. I would next read chapter(s) in my Bible, and then I would listen to His Words from a CD on the same chapter(s) that I had just read. I would then follow up and listen to the CD again by itself. Next, I would then pray. Can you imagine all of this being done before I go to work at 6:00 a.m. in the morning?

I also chose not to go to sleep at night without doing a few things as well, because God was more important than extra minutes of sleep. My dad said this better about sleeping, "Only thing comes to a sleeper, but a dream." Therefore, before I went to sleep I would read over some chapters and verses and began memorizing some of the verses. Alongside, I would read over His Commandments every night before I went to sleep. Since I knew how powerful the tongue is, I decided to read aloud God's Laws. This will ensure that His Words would not only be released in the atmosphere, but also be spoken into existence. Then I would pray or vice versa each night, in no particular order.

Of course, I did not stop there. I continued to go a step further by increasing my prayer life. I was part of the prayer team that met once a week. I was also part of a Book Group that met once a month at church, and I started doing a Book Mission for God. I started attending Bible Study during the week. I was now more than just a weekend warrior. In addition, I also helped, when needed, at different types of community functions.

Just stop and marinate on it for a moment, the reason that time is just as vital as money is because we all have it. Regardless of our status, whether we are rich, poor, young, old, overweight, or underweight. God gives us all time. He gives the same amount of the time of a day to everyone. How we make use of that time is really the key.

Just knowing all of these things previously mentioned, our relationship with God should be even better than a marriage. We should never ever want to stop loving God and always want Him to be our "1" and only God and Father. We should be real when we worship God in spirit; and let it come from deep down inside of our hearts and our minds should be totally devoted on Him.

We should not only be eager to make a daily sacrifice to God, but be willing to sacrifice all that we have to glorify God. We cannot be too quick to judge others by our standards and not examine ourselves for the things we have put first before God. Those things, whether it was money, friends, family, houses, liquor, cell phones, sexual activities, cars, drugs, so-called gods, etc. can definitely not save us from our sins. If we do not start taking the courage to acknowledge God, and put Him foremost in everything that we do, and before all others, God will show us firsthand who the real living God truly is.

Chapter 2

IDOLS FREE

Can you take a quick moment and look at some of the things that are in your house or either surrounding your house? In addition, while you are doing this go ahead and think about that person(s) you stated that you could not live without in your life. Next, contemplate on all the times that you spend unnecessarily going over and beyond with that particular thing(s) or person(s). Yes, you got it! The ones that you are idolizing and giving more of your attention to instead of God. Nevertheless, just in case you had to struggle a little bit deciding on some things let me go ahead and help you some. How about your car, shoes, drugs, television, situations, food, problems, job, clothes, cell phone, illness, money, internet, sexual activities, liquor, a particular person, credit cards, yourself, sodas, and whatever else you can name. These things, that you have dedicated yourself to can be detrimental, not only to your mind but also to your body. Have you noticed how much time and devotion that you have given to them in comparison to the little time, or no time, that you have spent with God, or the lack of praise that you are given God?

"Little children, keep yourselves from idols. Amen" *(1 John 5:21).* We need to stay away from anything that will keep us from loving God to the fullest. Okay, you want to go a little deeper into this? How about worshiping and cherishing people who we call our favorite heroes, stars, athletes, etc. until we begin to idolize them? We have put them so high up on a pedestal until they have reached the sky. God commanded us to be idols-free. We need to stop the worshiping of heroes, athletes, stars, etc., and oh, let us not forget the dead that we are worshipping. We

need to give God all the glory and the honor that He deserves.

When I contemplated the meaning of the word jealous, I believe "a jealous God" was used because we are familiar with the meaning of being jealous far too well. We know from all the different types of events that have happened in our lives whether from a childhood standpoint, a friend, a sibling, or a spouse, etc. We can easily relate to the meaning of being able to be faithful to only one individual. Just think about it, what if your children go against you and they start loving, obeying, and doing for another individual other than you? You would be angry and start getting a little jealous. That love and hate syndrome. You would consider your children as being disloyal. In addition, you would view them as being disrespectful and not having no consideration of you, the one who birth them, and everything else you have done for them. God is like this in the same manner. He is also caring and protective.

In addition, let's look at it from another angle. I believe the word jealous was used to show how serious God really is not about worshiping and giving praises to something or someone else besides Him. God want us to know upfront that He is not going to have it. He will not let us cheat on Him by loving other gods. You would feel the same way if someone you cared deeply about hurt you.

When it comes to God, some say that they cannot worship in Spirit, but let somebody die. We talk to them continuously, morning, noon, and night. We would then say, "I hope that he or she can hear me" or "I know that they are watching over me." Therefore, that in itself proves that we can worship in spirit. That is why it is so "very-very" serious about giving God all the praise and worship. God is not a play toy, and not to be played with. Whatever we're going to do in life, we will be disciplined for our actions. The consequences will not only apply to us, but our children, grandchildren, and our great-grandchildren. This also sometimes applies to people within our vicinity and not just to us being punished for our actions. Just as in a jealous relationship after an individual has stated that they love you then turns around and brings disaster on you in a hateful way. This meant that good and evil happened to you by that same person. A similar situation occurs when we are obedient or disobedient to God. There is some good and evil that will come into a relationship. There is some good if we do obey and if we do not obey, then there will be some evilness that will come upon us. God will release His covering. You will be left into the hands of your enemies. You may even die!

We have to be careful not to idolize things and/or persons. When it comes to worshiping God, we act as if we do not have time for God. Our footprints are nowhere to be found close to a church. However, we find time to spend all day to adore our cars (no mechanical issues), browse the internet (no apparent reason), go shopping (have abundant clothes and shoes). Some of us also do the same thing by idolizing our children and obeying their directive to the letter more than we do God's Commandments. It took Sarah a long time to have a child, but Abraham still did not put his son before God. Abraham was considered righteousness by being obedient and willing to give his son back to God for a sacrifice and by having faith he knew that God would provide. He did both; he demonstrated his faith and he took action. He loved God. Not like some of us. We tend to forget what all God has done for us and then we leave Him on the back burner.

Today things have changed in so many ways. We now leave the children at the house and we go to church. They were not too sleepy to watch television, or be on the internet, etc. We should all be going to church on a regular basis. We have to get back that attitude that everyone in my house will serve and give God the glory. Do not let our cell phone guide us. We keep up with it more than we do our Bible. Nowadays we cannot leave home without our cell phones! If we noticed, after getting to work that we have left our cell phone at home; we'll leave work, and go home to get it. We find an excuse; that we need it just in case the car breaks down, or that we're waiting on an important phone call that we cannot miss. Let me remind you that you may have already missed that important call, and you have just risked the car being broken down while going back home. It is funny how God had us then when we returned to go and get our cell phone. Let's stop getting the big head thinking that we do everything ourselves, and not forgetting that it is God that does and give us everything we need including our life itself.

<u>**My Sacrifice:**</u> *The first thing that I normally did when I walked into the house was turn on the television set and the last thing that I did before going to bed was watching television. This was something I was doing on a daily basis just like clockwork. I wasn't realizing it had actually became a habit. It had became my pastime. I had to stop giving my television too much glory.*

I had to turn this whole concept around. I decided that I wanted God to be the first thing that was on my mind in the morning, and the last thing on my mind at night. I wanted my thoughts to be more focused toward God.

In reality, I guess you can say that the television was becoming my god. I was serving the television. No, I did not bow down to it, but I was worshiping it and spending more time with it than with God. It was becoming more important than God. It was where my heart was. I was enjoying all my free and valuable time with the television. I had to see all of my favorite shows, which became more and more shows instead of spending more time with God. I decided to start limiting my television watching time to the weekends and one day during the week. I reduced it further while I attended school; to one day on the weekend, and one day during the week to ensure I spent more time with God.

I can also recall the times when I used to joke around when someone did something spectacular. I used to bend down my head to them as a joke (I know you may do it too!), not realizing and unaware that what I was actually doing was going through the motion of bowing down to them as if they were God. Of course, I was laughing about it. However, do you think God was laughing and thinking it was funny too? I should not have pretended to bend down or raise my arms as if I was worshiping them and giving them the honor. Instead I decided just to clap my hands for them for a job well done.

I had to change my mindset and my whole thought process. My whole heart would have to be worshiping God, and only God, regardless if I was playing around or being serious. Some of us think that we have gotten clever in a new way of building altars. Even though no one can physically see them, but we are building the so-called altars in our mind. We think about and worship these so-called gods day and night. Our minds are being corrupted. We are dying each day by guns, bad health (over and under eating), and various diseases mostly due to idolizing our cars, televisions, sports, food, clothes, money, people, etc. God takes this very serious because some have even died suddenly by being disobedient, and not being idol-free. We have to make it our responsibility to obey God's Commandments by putting God first, and giving Him all the praise and honor that He deserves and not giving it to anyone or nothing else. It is time for us to be witnesses and tell the world about the God that we serve, worship, trust, and love.

Chapter 3

NAME OF GOD INAPPROPRIATE

Often times we say some things that we should not have said. Even though it could have been our intent to actually use it in a good way or in a way that was not harmful to anyone. Later on, we wish that we could take it all back. The fact remains that we still have used it in an inappropriate manner. The reasoning does not matter; whether it was done purposely, or accidentally when it comes to God's name. We should not use God's name in vain.

The way we use God's name should be according to God's standard and not how we think we should be using His name. If we do misuse God's name, we will be held accountable. Depending on what was said, it could be used to vindicate us or to condemn us. With that being stated, we should never blaspheme the name of God. God's name should not be associated in any kind of cruel or vicious way. We should be able to put a lid on our tongue when speaking; if not, it shows that our so call religion is in vain and we are only lying to ourselves. If people curse out each other, God will be the judge. We will have to give an account for it. If we curse God, and God is the all mighty judge, we are asking for a death sentence.

In addition, we should not have to prove ourselves by making a point by using God's name inappropriately. Even though there may be some jobs that have you swear holding your hands up. They get you to say, "So help me God." Wait a minute, how about in court? When we say yes and no that should be the end of our response to answer someone. This should be suffice and nothing more should be added on to it. We should not have to swear and say it in God's name. Otherwise, we would be using God's name unfittingly. Our yes should be yes and our no should be no.

Using God's name this way has been done for such a long time that now, we do not even think twice about it.

By using God's name inappropriately, we are still unable to change the outcome of anything by swearing to it. No, only God can do that. *"But I say unto you, Swear not at all; neither by heaven; for it is God's throne" (Matthew 5:34):* God regulates what happens in our life. We do not have the power to do anything without Him. Yes, no promises should be made by using God's name in vain. Only God knows if we are really being honest or not. It is all in God's Hands. He is the Master of all things, not us.

My Sacrifice: *It only took a second to know what I needed to stop doing. I am as guilty as the above. A habit needed to be broken immediately. If you do not believe me, no I am not going to confirm it and say, "So help me God," or "I say that I would put my hands on the Bible." That is what I had to stop saying. Therefore, I did! I gave it up. Whatever my answer was that's what it was. I will not be reassuring with using God's name inappropriate in any kind of a way. It was a small sacrifice to make, but a powerful one as I began to watch closely what I say.*

Since it is best for us not to swear at all, we all have to do a better job of controlling what we do and say. We should be using our mouth to worship God's name and giving Him honor that comes from our hearts. How can we worship and praise God with the same breath and tongue that we curse out each other, as we are all in the same image of God? Since the power is in the tongue, we have to be careful about what things we say with our tongue because it could backfire on us and become a curse to us.

By using our tongue to say wicked stuff out of our mouths, we are only worshipping Satan and giving him the glory. We should not be lip-syncing by worshipping with our lips saying, "Oh my God", as if we are so holy, but our heart is not right with God. Do not say God's name when there is no purpose or apparent reason by joking around using God's name thoughtless. The use of God's name is now being carried on a little thick, and now some say it and use it as a joke. Some people might say, "You need God" as a joking matter just to get a few laughs. Stop using God's name in vain! If that person needs God then we need to be serious and start praying for that individual. How will they come to God when they see that we are not serious?

You definitely do not want to be cursing and speaking God's name in the same sentence. Sometimes I hear people use the name of God and a curse word in the same sentence. There were no apologies afterwards. We have to stop disrespecting the name of God. Some say they love God then turn around and slam the door in the face of His children. In addition, we have to be careful about what's on our mind. We may be thinking evil thoughts while in church and saying Hallelujah all at the same time. In addition, we may be reading our Bible and thinking of whom about the next person we will conquer and lay down with tonight, or thinking of doing something evil to someone. We need to ask God for forgiveness right now. Better yet, how can we say we love God when we treat others hatefully? Wake up God's sheep, and let's treat everyone like we would like to be treated, with love and kindness.

Make sure that even our walk is not in vain. We should be genuine throughout the day, even when someone is not watching. We have to set an example that we are Godlike and not just playing church. We should not be hating on others even when a disobedient individual seem to be prospering more than we are. Their triumph is temporary. We have to keep our faith in God that we will prosper too. We should stay real with God regardless of our circumstances. Our mouth should be used as an encourager and a vindicator rather than a condemer by

You Want to Stop Sinning...Stop

saying evil things. We should go out our way to use God's name in an appropriate manner. It should be used only for the purpose of good. Normally, when something bad comes out of our mouth it is a reflection of what's in our heart. Do not be caught saying God's name in vain because it is a reflection of more than just who we are. Someone else is listening too you besides God. You never know who else overheard you and will mimic on what you have just said.

Chapter 4

OTHER AGREEMENTS

Most of us are familiar with the Ten Commandments, but are we aware of other guidelines that God wants us to observe as well. He has given us other agreements throughout the Bible of what He would do and what He wanted us to do. Is it okay with my readers, if I take this detour to share a few of the agreements with you? Better yet, try to see if you are familiar with any of them.

Some of the agreements established by God are to last forever. Yes, they were made permanent. Do not forget that God does not lie. In addition, we have to keep in mind that Jesus did not come to abolish the Commandments, but to see them through. Now here is a good one for you. If you look up in the sky shortly after it has been raining you may see a rainbow. Do you know what it signifies? Yes, it is pretty, but it is so much more than beautification. When I see this lovely colorful rainbow, it's a reminder that God is confirming and putting His stamp on the agreement that He made with us. *"I do set my bow in the cloud, and it shall be for a token of a covenant between me and the earth" (Genesis 9:13).* God made an everlasting agreement that He will set a rainbow in the cloud to symbolize that He will not cause a flood to destroy the whole earth again. Okay, great, you might have known that one, but I had to mention it anyway.

Here is another one. How many of you like to eat your steak or hamburger medium-rare. Yes, there are quite a few of you. Did you know that it is a permanent agreement between God and us that we do not eat anything with blood in it? The reason for this is that the blood is the lifeline. We wonder why we act the way we do; being aggressive and hard to control our emotions. Think about it!!!! (Hint) Did we turn into what we have just eaten?

You Want to Stop Sinning...Stop

So far, you are saying, "oh I knew those." Okay, this next particular agreement is not only an everlasting agreement, but it is also a Commandment. Did you know that? There will be more discussion on this Commandment in a later chapter. This agreement signified that God is the Lord that blesses us and He is the only God. The agreement I am referencing is the agreement that God made about the Sabbath day should be holy unto the Lord. Out of six days of the week, God worked and made Heaven, earth, and sea. He rested on the seventh day of that week. It didn't state He was tired and rested. He relaxed. He took one day of the week off. God wants us to allow time to glorify and appreciate Him for all the things that He has done for us, and not what we have done with our hands. We have to take time out to taste how sweet life is and how great God is.

Okay now I know you are ready for this next one. This one is about tithing. Some of us are probably waiting on doing this one when we get more money or get richer. If we all wait until then, we may not ever give. God has done a lot for us. I know we cannot repay Him for all He has done, but we can start by showing gratitude.

It is time for us to start giving back to the Originator. Of course, you know some of us still do this today; but I had contemplated this. It had appeared to me more and more that the net amount was my first fruit and that I was supposed to be giving that amount. I really did not see in actuality any of the money until after the withholdings and other miscellaneous items had been taken out of my salary. Now, you know I had to rationalize this even farther. I started getting technical. The net amount of my pay was the availability of the amount of funds that I have in my hands. Similarly, if it were actually fruits, I would not be giving the rotten ones, just the ripe ones. Neither would I have considered the fruits that may have fallen out my basket on the ground, just the ones that I brought with me to give back.

On the flip side of this, we do not need to think that tithing and offering are important. We can be as Ananias and his wife in which they held back some of the money for God from sale of their land. Do you know what happen to them? Or else, we can be faithful like Jacob and give God 10% of all that we have. Elaborating on all of this made me recall when I was youngster walking to church. Mom gave me some money for church. There was a store right before you get to church. I spent some of the money to buy some candy. I put what was leftover in the church bucket. No, I was not struck by lightning, thank goodness for God's mercy!! Oh, when mom found out what I did, I did get a whipping. It is important that we give God our truthful tithes, which is holy unto the Lord. This is what I had to make up in my mind to do. I wanted to make genuine sacrifices to God rather than give Him my leftovers, my donation, or giving just to receive a deduction.

<u>My Sacrifice</u>: *I decided to tithe regardless of my financial situation. I thought about it long and hard and speculated on which was the correct way the Lord really intended for me to give back. I asked myself whether it was from the gross or the net amount of my income. I had to take a step back and then realized that I was not giving either way.*

At first I started giving only ten percent from the net amount of my paycheck. However, I was actually giving God my leftovers so I wanted to be on the safe side and do right by God. But I wanted to be sure so I began giving my tithe from the gross amount of my income. I knew that I couldn't go wrong by giving Him my best. I started using the bill pay process to treat my tithes just as important as if was a bill. I made sure God was paid first before any other bills.

You Want to Stop Sinning...Stop

What it all boils down to is that God had already provided me with the money that I had. I was just giving back what He actually had given me. I knew that it was not as if God actually needed it. God has everything! It's just another way to see if we do not mind giving Him our all. It also keeps us humble, knowing that we did not get this money on our own. It teaches us to share and not to be so selfish with our blessings.

This is still a growing process for us, we get an opportunity to develop our trust in Him. We take a chance that He will provide for all our every need. It goes to show that when we do what is right and be faithful in doing it, the Lord will bless us. One of the best things that happened after I tithed and paid my bills was realizing I still had some money left afterwards. My funds were not as skimpy as before. Is not God awesome?

Some may be thinking that the priest is not doing what is right with the tithes. Do not use that as a cop-out. No, we just have to do what is right. God will take care of the priests if they are doing wrong by using the tithes unwisely and sinfully. We have to remember that God wanted them to have it especially to use for the upkeep of the church as well as their inheritance. When we do not give God what is due to Him, the money in our pockets will be like a pocket with a big hole in it. We can't keep it. There will always be something we think we need it for, someone taking it, or we will always be indebted to others.

In addition, by us tithing, we are giving honor to God for all the blessings we have received. Yes, the tithe is 10% of the gross amount of any income. That's right, you got it. This includes any type of refund you receive or money you found under the car seat. Both are God's blessings for which we should be thankful.

There are other guidelines and agreements that are in the Bible for us to be mindful of, such as the Passover (Israelites' houses), the Lord's Release (cancel debt), and many more. Some may think that they are now obsolete. If so, that may be the reason why things are not changing in our lives. We are not full-hearted following the agreements that are in the Bible to the best of our abilities. One of the statutes mentioned in the Bible is to ensure that we do not forget the Lord our God. Some things, such as, our eyebrows and the marks in the palm of our hands (look like an "M", "K" or etc.) were meant to be symbolic to remind us that one night the Lord our God was the one that brought the Israelites out of Egypt. Jesus also did not come to eliminate the Commandments handed down to this world; but to teach us all about God's great Kingdom. Those were just some of the agreements mentioned beforehand that were made between God and our ancestors for us to follow from generations to generations. The agreements were done out of love and His compassionate feeling towards us. However, we do have to fly right and turn from our evil ways. We should not want to die in our sins. If we follow His agreement and Commandments, God will not forget us or put us to everlasting death.

The Bible should be used to familiarize ourselves with God's Agreements and Commandments. God has given us the Bible as a guide to use with instructions of what to do-and-don't do regarding His laws and agreements. God stated in His Word that all His laws would be planted in our hearts and minds. It will be all part of our D.N.A. We have to keep our hearts and minds opened and listen to God when He talks to us in the spirit. We have to listen closely to what God is telling us and take heed. We have to know Him personally for ourselves. We have to be loyal to God and acquaint ourselves with His permanent Agreements and Commandments that God handed down to us. We have to be compliant to them and be joyful in them.

Chapter 5

A DAY OF REST

God is the one who created us and who knows us better than anyone. Yes, even ourselves. God designed our body so He knows what is required of us in order to function properly. God requested us to have one special day to rest in honor of Him and to keep it holy. God Himself rested after six days of work after He created this world. It was not because He had to, but to set an example for us to follow.

If you pay close attention to the Bible, some of the Ten Commandments have a brief statement regarding them. For examples, do not kill or do not steal. While the fourth Commandment about the Sabbath is much wordier, and has more than one sentence to it, do you think this particular one may be of some importance? Especially since more information and emphasis was given to it than the other Commandments. Could this also be because this Commandment is a permanent agreement between God and us that signifies that He is the one and only God that blesses us? Or else, could this be because this particular Commandment should not be taken likely? Keep in mind this is also one of the easiest Commandments to do. It is just that simple. You do n-o-t-h-i-n-g. Nothing...not a thing!! You rest. God asked us to keep it holy. We should do everything we can to make this day peaceful. It should be a joyful day. We should go out our way to be nice, especially on this holy day. There should be no mourning on this day. Neither should we be sad on this day. We have to turn those ill feelings away! We have to be glad on this day that God has made holy.

We often put everything before God, even our jobs. We think that our job cannot do without us. News flash!! Do die tomorrow and see what happens on our job.

Remember we are suppose to be the one that they cannot do without at all. Believe me, the work will still go on without us. Matter of fact our death may not get a moment of silence. They might say that this is what he or she would have done or wanted us to do, and then continue on working.

"And they returned, and prepared spices and ointments; and rested the sabbath day according to the commandment" (Luke 23:56). Yes, the New Testament does acknowledge the Sabbath Day. Now for those that had doubted, this means that the Sabbath still should be obeyed. Do we do it? Most of us do not. Do we try? The same goes there too. Most of us do not.

I know, I hear you. You may think how can we rest on the Sabbath Day, that most of us call Sunday, go to church, and give God the praise and honor when our employer requires us to work on that day? Your point has been taken. Maybe the churches need to go back and model after how Peter and the other disciples taught in the church and people's houses daily regarding Jesus Christ. Yes, people were able to get the Word more than just on Sundays. God asked us to only work six days in a week and one day was to be holy and for rest. God knows us too well. We need to stop giving excuses not to rest. He even knew that we may have rested ourselves, but told everybody else in the house to work. Ha!! Ha!! That's why He emphasized that no one or nothing in your household should work that day. Okay, since God asked for one day, then we need to go ahead, and take one day of the week to rest, and make it holy. God knows your situation.

God is the one that blesses us. It is not our job, bank account, family members, friends, etc. God requested for our body and mind to take a break and rest so that we can bounce back. It makes you wonder if this is the reason why so many people go insane or become unhealthy, because there was no sufficient rest of their mind and body?

    <u>**My Sacrifice**</u>: *I was working full time and going to school. I observed that I was spending a lot of my time doing homework and putting it before God, at least it was how I devoted my time. I thought that there was not enough time in the day or in the week to accomplish all of the things that I wanted to do. Nevertheless, I was so determined to finish them all. How could I possibly take a little breather from all the things that I had to finish? What it all sounded like was that I knew what was better for me than God? I finally decided to take a halt in all the things that I was doing. I started resting on the seventh day. I was determined to keep the Sabbath day holy as God requested. No, I was not going to work nor do any school homework on that day.*

    I decided that all of my job duties and school homework would have to be done on the other six days of the week. Regardless of how long it took, but not on Sundays. This change required more discipline from me. I had to come to a halt and shut it down right before midnight on Sundays regardless rather my homework was finished or not (fyi…graduated magna cum laude).

    I can now see clearer why the Lord asked for us to rest one day a week from all our works. After I had put this into practice for a while I felt more refresh for the upcoming week. I was rejuvenated. It felt that I had added years to my life. I was well rested. The resting period allowed me to be able to start my Monday mornings with the feeling that I could take on the world.

    I was giving back the seventh day to the Lord just what He had given me. I learned to relax and refocus. It was time for me to let my mind be open to listen to God. To help me honor God even more with resting I was not shopping at all the stores and neither shopping for grocery. I was also determined to try not to go out to eat on

You Want to Stop Sinning...Stop

Sundays. I did not want to be involved with anyone working for me on that day either. I wanted to make sure I did not make a mistake and misinterpret His Commandment. I started preparing my meals the day before or making sure that I had already bought what I wanted to eat for that day.

I knew the Sabbath Day must be serious business because no one or nothing should work, not even the animals nor the strangers are to work on our premises. Just think about it, you can control what's going on within your own house. It is difficult to control what other people do in their houses. Do not think God does not know the difference between us being greedy and us having no other choice but to work since the boss would not let us off. If we are just being greedy, we have to put more of our trust in God knowing that He will provide. All of God's sheep have to wake up now.

God wants us to stop whatever work we are doing and put Him first. Yes, our job and school have to be put to a halt to honor of God. Who knows what we need better than God? Why not show God that He is "numero uno." Yes, work can do without us for one day of the week.

God commanded us to work only six days and rest one day of the week. The funniest thing is that we still cannot do that. Could God be trying to teach us to slow down and to learn patience as well? On the other hand, could He be teaching us to enjoy life and do not let precious moments pass us by? We only have to rest in honor of God for one day out of the week. Simple, easy to grip, huh...that is what we all have been saying and thinking.

Chapter 6

VALUE AND OBEY YOUR PARENTS

God wants us to be obedient without a doubt. However, the practice of obedience begins first by obeying our parents. When I was younger, mom told me things not to do and I knew not to do them. That groundwork that I learned from being obedient to my mom carried me over even when I became an adult. Our parents have to exercise discipline when we misbehave or when we do not obey their instructions. God has to do the same thing when we misbehave or when we do not obey His instructions. God commanded us to honor our parents. This may be what we may want to call a practice test. How can we honor Him, who we cannot see with our two eyes if we cannot even honor our parents who are right there smack in front of our face?

The best one thing to remember is that when our parents do chastise us it does not mean that they do not care for us or do not love us. A matter of fact is that it means that they most definitely care and love us. Our parents did not want the wickedness of this world to get control over us. That is why they set rules and expected us to follow them. They did not want us to become selfish and start thinking that we can have everything our way and have whatever we want. We had to take the punishment our parents had in store for us. This chastisement helped us further down the road in our life. This is the same way it is with God about chastising. The chastising is going to come because He loves us as well, and it will help us on down the road.

God wants our hearts right so we should not mind obeying His Commandments. God wants us to be grateful, knowing that He is the one that gives us everything. He gives us our food, clothes, house, and yes, he even gives us our parents. Regardless of what we may think of them, our parents come from God.

Many of us can recall how our parents often said, "Make sure you stay away from any kids that are doing wrong". Do not think for even half of a second that it was because they did not trust you. No, it was far more than that. It was because they knew that their evil spirit could jump on you just by being around them. If you do not think this is doable, remember how the spirits came from the man and jumped onto the pigs or when the man was clean from the evil spirits and then more came back? Yes, the evil spirits do jump around from people to people and from place to place.

How do you think God feels about us when we do not listen to Him, especially when we already know He has our best interest at heart. This particular one of God's Commandment comes with a guarantee. *"HONOUR THY FATHER AND MOTHER; which is the first commandment with promise; THAT IT MAY BE WELL WITH THEE, AND THOU MAYEST LIVE LONG ON THE EARTH"* *(Ephesians 6:2-3).* You can see clearly that there is no stipulation mentioned here about "if" your parents happen to be great then obey them or, first they need to give you respect then you can obey them. God promised us if we obey our parents that He will extend our life. He would give us more days here on this earth. Wow, isn't this not a great proposal, that He will add years to our life if we obey our parents?

Since practicing obedience is best started from day one, yes, the younger is the better. I am not saying that we may not stumble along the way. For example, I was told at an early age to stay away from certain foods such as seafood and chocolate because they would break me out in a rash. I went back and forth doing the opposite of what mom had told me. I later learned it was best for me to be obedient for my good, and then I stopped and started being obedient to the fullest. It was really preparing me for some of the things I should stay away from today. We had to learn self-discipline being mindful and obedient to what our parents instructed us to do. This led us to having self-control. We have to know how to control our bodies and that includes our minds, our hands, and whatever else. When we get older we are then on our own and no one is going to tell us every step of the way what not to do or what to do. We are going to have to make a decision of when not to do something.

Parents do their best to provide for their children and ensure that there is food for them to eat. We are the same way today as the Israelites were with God, being ungrateful of what was given to them to eat. God had to humble the Israelites and therefore they had to spend 40 years in the wilderness. I have to say that I have also been ungrateful. I had to change my way of looking out for my own self-gratification, of wanting something different to eat, and not being grateful of what my mom had right there in front of me.

<u>My Sacrifice:</u> *One of the things I use to say when I was younger when my mom cooked chicken frequently, "We having chicken again. I am tired of eating chicken, fried chicken, boiled chicken, bake chicken, chicken salad, and chicken-chicken-chicken. If I eat another piece of chicken, I will probably turn into a chicken and may even fly away". Does this not sound familiar? If so, you were just like me, being ungrateful.*

I decided that I would make a change with my whole outlook on things and stop complaining. I had to take a step back and really analyze the situation. I realized that at least I had something to eat and there was food on the table. I decided that I would value and be more appreciative of what my mom had done. She had provided enough food for us to eat regardless of what type it is. I was not starving and going to bed hungry.

You Want to Stop Sinning...Stop

Sometimes we complain and it is unknown to us that we are doing all that moaning. If you do not think complaining is serious business, think again. Yes, think about what happened to the Israelites in the wilderness when they complained. They were lusting and reminiscing on what they ate in Egypt. God had fed them manna, yet they were ungrateful and not satisfied. A plague was brought against them. God had given them meat, but while the meat was still in their mouth, it began coming out of their noses and they died. This will make you stop and change the way you think about the seriousness of complaining and about being grateful for what you have. As I have gotten older, it makes me really appreciate and value what my parents have done for me even more. Also, be careful about saying what you cannot do without or what you want. God should be the only one you cannot do without and not food. Have you ever thought that maybe the reason why we have diabetes, high blood pressure, and heart attacks is because of lusting after food?

Even though it takes more than food to sustain us, our parents knew that we also need the Word of God to keep us alive. Not only reading His Words, but we also need to listen to what God is telling us. We have to walk truthful in doing the right thing and then trust that God will lead us in the right direction. Listen to Him then do what God wants you to do. Eventually you will start "wanting" to do right and wanting to be obedient without any hesitation.

Why do you think God gave parents leadership over their children? How many of us have the Ten Commandments posted in our home or maybe in our office? We should have the Commandments posted somewhere in our home. How many of us teach our kids to obey the Ten Commandments? We should not only obey them, but also know all of God's Commandments by heart. That should be a lesson taught to them just as much as do not touch a hot stove. We should be teaching not only our kids, but also our grandkids and so on. Then they will teach "their" children and grandchildren and so on. They should know how important God's directive is. We should continue to speak of the Commandments constantly and consistently. Are you wondering why you cannot resist your enemies? Don't you want power over your enemies? When you obey the Commandments whatever you do and everything you touch should prosper, but not only you, but also your entire household. You will be given peace. The Bible also should be our best past time book to read, to get more in tune to what God wants us to do, and to become better at it.

Parents are similar to managers in charge. They are the ones that are running the organization. It is funny how we can obey everyone else and do what they say but do except what our parents tell us to do. At times, children do not even humble themselves to respect the elderly. We all should be glad that times have changed and it is not like when the Israelites had disobedient children. They would chastise them, and if they would continue being disobedient they would later be stoned to death to get rid of the wickedness from around them. They did not want God to be angry with them.

The reason it is so hard on the children today is because some children are getting some of the repercussion of what our ancestors have done previously. In addition to repercussions to what they are doing which gives them a triple portion or more of trouble. We have to keep praying for them constantly. God wants to give us more blessings than He gave our parents, grandparents, or other ancestors as long as we are obedient and follow His Commandments.

When I started making sacrifices in my life, some of them didn't come easy; but they were more obtainable due to me being obedient to my parents. By following my parents' rules and regulations it made it easier to follow the commitments that I made to God. We should always want to be pleasing to God by honoring and valuing His Commandments and in return, we will be honoring and valuing our parents. Okay, perhaps you have not done so, but you're never too old to learn to be obedient. You can start right now.

Chapter 7

DO NOT PUT TO DEATH ANYONE

God commanded us not to murder one individual and there was no "if-statements" included. When we use "if-statements", we are all talking out the side of our necks. It does not matter what the so-called circumstances were. We all try to justify ourselves for killing someone especially when it was not an accident. Yeah, we know all quite too well about wicked Cain who killed his brother. Even today, nothing has changed, we are still killing our brothers. Okay, you're right. You got me. Only the names have changed. All of God's sheep have to wake up now. We think we can deviate how and when we want to obey this Commandment.

You may be saying when it best benefits us then it is okay to put someone to death. If you can recall, it is not just physically killing someone. It is so much deeper. It is also what's in our hearts and minds. With all that being stated, I would have to confess, I am guilty on all accounts. When we hate someone and then that's dealing with mentally killing someone. For example, hatred, it starts with killing one individual in your mind then it spreads like a disease until you have killed millions and millions of people. Then someone else may follow suit from observing how you have treated others. As a result, many people will begin not exhibiting kindness and love for one another. In essence, we would have killed a generation of people. Just like it is today. A whole generation of people is becoming loveless.

There are also the silent killers, which goes even deeper. Yes, I hear you loud and clear; that you never have pulled a trigger. Think again! Remember, I said silent killer. We are the ones behind the scenes. We are those that just happen to come up with the money. You know, the ones that paid someone to kill someone else. We might not have personally handed the money to them directly, but we may have been the ones that gave it to the person to give to them to do the killing. Okay, now you are stating that you still do not fall in that category. Then how about the one that came up with the so-called bright idea to kill them (hint...not referring to a type of assassin that is in a movie)? Yet, we are still a contracted killer. Once again, do not be too quick to judge. We have to remember that God knew us before we were formed in our mother's belly. The ones taking the pill the morning after, the ones taking the pills every day, the ones (male or female) that got the surgery, the ones that are the persuades to do those things, or anything that tries to keep God from performing one of His greatest miracles. Wake up God's sheep!!!

Okay, here is another category. You will know which category you fall under as you read these statements. For example, we are the ones that stated that they were going to die anyway or maybe their pain was unbearable. Or, we may think they have lived their life then we probably handed them over some pills or a needle. If not, then maybe we gave them something to drink, or put the bullets in the revolver for them. You got the picture. Just name it!

Let's not be too quick to judge another! They were still God's people. All of this equates to the fact that they were still killed and the hit was put on them. Yes, we had hired an assassin. It is even more awful when the hit was made on someone that did not have the capability of running or hiding. If they knew they probably would have hid somewhere we could not found them. Yet if the truth had really been told, we felt that we were justified by doing it. Once again, all of God's sheep have to wake up right this moment! There is no exception to God's rule about killing even if someone wants to die. Nor if someone is already dying, we cannot put him or her to death. Not even if that person is in pain. In those instances, it is really the time that we need to pray even more. It is the time to rely more on God. God will provide us with the peace we need in all these types of circumstances.

If we see someone being murdered, we have to testify, and get the guilt off our conscience. We testify even if we think we should not snitch. Let me ask you this; out of all the people in the world, why do you think the murder was done right before your eyes? You are not only just a witness, but also God's witness. We are God's mouthpiece here on this earth. It is up to us to tell what we have seen. We were there in plain sight to tell the truth. God has given us this duty to see how we are going to handle it. As God's sheep, it is our obligation to do what is right. That's one of the reasons why there is a lot of killing going on around us. We are seeing all this happening right under our noses and we are not doing anything about it. Do you not think for a second that someone is going to have to give an account for these killings?

"Ye have heard that it was said of them of old time, THOU SHALT NOT KILL: and whosoever, shall kill shall be in danger of the judgment" (Matthew 5:21): There should be no killing whether planned or unplanned, even though we might not be aware of who actually did the killing. When blood is shed in our city then that blood is not only on the head of the person that did the killing, but it is also a reflection on the whole city. The city has been contaminated with this evilness. We should not want to bring all this sin on our city, which may result in bringing more evilness upon it. Are you wondering why some cities are one of top leaders on the murder rate chart? It is because the city has opened up the door to killings and left it wide open to more of these types of issues. We have to feed God's sheep by letting them know that it is wrong when they do not divulge what they have witnessed. This has to end now!

You Want to Stop Sinning...Stop

It is so important that we do not take killing someone lightly. We should not want to hurt anyone enough to kill them. It is awful to say, but we'd rather kill one another than look at each other. God stated that more than one witness is needed for capital punishment. We should all have one common goal, and no one should be out for him or herself. We are quick to say that a person did this or did that to us and then feel we have to get back at the person for what they have done. We should not take any part in revenge by killing each other. I remember my elderlies often stated that we should not be killing someone dog because he or she had killed our cat. God is the one that will pay back that individual according to their sins for not following God's Commandments. Now, it's a scary thing to be paid back by God. Nowadays the killers do not care whom they kill. They do not have a conscience. There are no boundaries set. The killers do not have any respect, not even for the elderly. Nor do they show any pity for the kids. However, they will be punished for what they done.

We have to find ways to control our mind and our body. Exercise is one of the things that can help to reduce stress and keep us from being so hostile towards one another. Take it from me; you will be able to better control your mind and body. By exercising, you will be too tired to act irrationally and will not want to think about hurting anyone. You will want to just lie down and get some rest.

My Sacrifice: *I decided to make a change on the way I think. I was determined to be better manage my thought patterns and not to be extremely angry with anyone. This would help keep a brotherly love attitude. I was taught a long lesson at an early adult age that you should not get too angry with anyone. As mom better stated that: taught sense was better than bought sense, and bought sense was better than none at all. You should keep the peace and walk away. I learned not to carry hate* *inside me against anyone even if someone had ill feelings toward me or had done me wrong. I was determined to practice good anger management.*

In addition, I was also determined there would be no ill remarks from me of any kind regarding any type of alternatives as to whether someone should live or die rather young or old regardless of their circumstances. I decided to keep my heart right and in tune with God's wants, not my own selfish wants or opinions. By doing this, my whole mind concept changed the way I see and do things and I had a better look on life for God's glory.

We need to stop helping with putting all the afflictions on us by keeping the wicked activities from around us. God's land is being defiled by all the killing. An amends has to be made for all the killings whether we have done it or not especially if we saw who did it. Remember, we are still guilty if we saw the killing but did not tell who did it. We have helped to defile the land by not telling and we are the ones who have to answer to God. We should not be scared of what man can do to us. God does not teach us to be fearful. We have to ask God for forgiveness even though we did not do it. When we do we will be helping our cities, states, even the world regarding all of this wickedness.

We should never stop praying and asking God for the ability to have the desire to keep praying. There is always something or someone to pray for regardless of who you are. When you pray it does not always have to be about yourself. It does not matter if we know or not know who did it, or why it was done. We still need to ask God for forgiveness for everyone; and yes, this will be showing the unconditional love that we should have for each other.

At other times, we tend to want to play as if we were God. For example we may think they did not have long to live, they are getting too expensive, they have already lived their life, or I do not want them to be in pain.

You Want to Stop Sinning…Stop

Then we start rationalizing. If it was me, then I would not want to live. I stated it earlier and I will state it again, "Wake up." We are not God. That is a decision that God makes and not us. When it is time for us to go, and not until then, He will take us. Whatever type of disguised killer you may be, or if you are involved in killing someone, or watch and do nothing we are all still guilty. The good news is that God will forgive us. We have to ask God to pardon our sins. For whatever the reason, we may have thought that the outlook would not be promising, and therefore we did what we did. Don't be like Abimelech who killed his seventy brothers out of greed and for prestige. There are no "if" clauses for intentional killings. Let God do His work. God is still in the miracle business. He has the final say-so. Just be obedient to His Word and do not kill. When we are obedient we can see how peaceable it will be and how much rest God's will gives us here on Earth.

CHAPTER 8

A DEMAND FOR BEING SICK-FREE

It is truly amazing how some things will work out for our good. If we just do what God ask us to do. God demanded us to obey His Commandments and in return He will keep diseases from us. Yes, we could be sick-free. Of course, there is a flip side to all this as well. One thing you can be sure about, if we do not follow His Commandments, there will be consequences. God could allow various illnesses, not only to have an affect our lives, but it could also affect our children and our children's children until we are completely wiped out from the earth.

Our bodies are amazingly made. When we are sick, our bodies are talking back to us trying to inform us of something. Listen!! Listen!!! It is telling us to stop doing what we are doing and do what is right according to God's eyes. It is revealing to us that we may need to do something as simple as to rest. Let it be known that we need to cut back on those long hours at work. Even if we overindulge, we still may be hungry after eating. We will not be satisfied due to all the barricades due to our sins. Sometimes when we get an illness, it may be telling us to stop eating all of that junk food. Yep, you also may need to ask yourself this one too; when was the last time you laid off all that meat, processed or not? All of this could even mean we may need to get into a closer relationship with God and worship Him. *"And ye shall serve the Lord your God, and he shall bless thy bread, and thy water; and I will take sickness away from the midst of thee" (Exodus 23:25).* During the period of sickness is when (most of time) we want God's special attention. We normally talk to Him then, and ask for His help. God will bless us in so many awesome ways if we just worship Him only. He will even keep us from being infertile, and that goes for any animals we may have also.

Have you ever thought about other people when you are in church getting ready to eat the Lord's Supper? We may reflect on God's Word that many are sick among us due to eating and drinking the Lord's Supper unworthily. Some do not eat and drink the Lord's Supper thinking that they are unworthy to eat and drink it. If that were the case no one would be praiseworthy or excellent enough to consume it. The Word states unworthily, which has a different meaning. You just have to be genuine and sincere when eating and drinking it. We just need to be serious about the concept, and that's why there should be no talking, texting, no clowning around, etc. during the Lord's Supper presentation because it is regarding the gospel of Jesus.

God is a healer. If we follow His Commandments, He will take all the diseases from us. He stated that we would not get any of the diseases that the Egyptians had. Think about it for a moment. Have you ever heard or read of Jesus having any illness or even a cold? Jesus was all about our Father's business. The way we should be. Jesus knew we could not be perfect, that's why He mentioned that there was only one who was perfect and that was God. We should be all about God's business.

I started reminiscing of what a previous doctor stated to me. About eight years ago the doctor stated that I had asthma. I stated to her that I had played basketball morning, noon, and night when I was younger. How could I be? I played all the time. She stated that some things you acquire when you are older. She gave me a prescription for an asthma inhaler. In addition, she stated that my blood pressure was a little bit high also. She gave me some medication for it. After taking it for a few days, the high blood pressure medication had me unable to urinate. I knew then something was not right, and that this was not for me. I was not going to give in to this, nor claim it. I was thinking more and more about the situation of having asthma and that I could die in a moment by not breathing. Then I had to realize that I had to take a step back. I said to myself, "Wake up!" God is the one in control of my breathing anyway. I was getting it all twisted. It did not just start now. God was in control of my breathing from day one and everything else regardless of the situation. I have often heard, many times, to do what the doctor said. How about us doing what God says? Based on my past I knew that God had my back then and He definitely got me now.

I was going to make a liar out of the devil. I kept my faith in God and kept reading His Word, praying, and doing God's work. I knew my body having asthma and high blood pressure was in God's hand. My relationship with God had gotten deeper and deeper. I was sick-free from the asthma and high blood pressure. I wanted to continue to keep my body uncontaminated from both the inside and the outside. Therefore, I went a step further and started changing some of my bad habits. All of this led me into my next sacrifice. I did not want anything to slow me down from doing God's work.

My Sacrifice: *Now these sacrifices coincided with me wanting to continue to be sick-free as well as obedient to God's Laws as stated in His Word. I decided to give up my leisure time to do something more beneficial to take care of my body. I wanted to thank God for allowing me to be sick-free and to show that I cared enough about my body to start taking care of it. Therefore, I started back exercising. I became more than a weekend warrior. I was exercising 3-5 days a week. I do have to admit though, it was a great challenge at first, especially, since I was older. The more I stuck with the regimen the better the process became. Oh yeah, during the week I was still* *about our Father's business. However, I was more energized.*

In addition, I made a decision not to eat meat. This came from meditating on the Book of Daniel. I started eating fruits, vegetables, and drinking water only. This is what God had originally given us to eat. Not only did I lose some weight, my skin was much smoother than ever before. The most out of all the changes that I noticed was that my memorization was better. I could remember more things. I was able to think faster on my feet just like I had done when I was younger.

My trial period was finally up. The holidays were approaching. Therefore, I decided to make a bigger challenge and extended this experimentation past the holidays. Yes, I was able to endure, but not through just any old holidays. It was through the most consumption holidays. Yes, can you just imagine going through Thanksgiving and Christmas without eating meat (Ha! Ha!). Then later, I extended it even further. I was able to sustain because I was grateful for the food that I was eating and I did not focus on what I was not eating.

Just think about this for a moment, out of all of the meats that we can eat in the world. Why do we love eating beef, such as, steaks, hamburgers, etc.? Especially knowing that this is parallel to the golden calf the Israelites worshiped as a god and made sacrifices to as an idol. Do you think God wants us to be eating a cow that was used symbolically for a god?

Both of those sacrifices that I made helped to keep my temple uncontaminated both inside and out. Go ahead, try it, and do not be like some others that stated that they could not do without meat, or do not have enough time in the day to exercise. Manoah's wife was childless. By putting God first, she had Samson, one of the strongest men ever and who would save the Israelites. However, she had to first abstain from eating and drinking certain things. So don't say what you cannot do without. It is all about God's work and pleasing Him, not ourselves. What better way to do God's work by keeping our bodies uncontaminated? I was later transformed. I was in a deeper relationship with God.

God has blessed me as I have not been on any daily meds for over eight years and I have not had any problems. I was told by my current doctor that I made him mad in a joking way because I did not have any problems and that nothing was bothering me. My blood pressure was good. Yes, and being over the hill and through the woods a little bit, I still exercise three to five days a week. God is good, better than that. God is great! My relationship with God got deeper. I could see the changes in me both inside and outside. I am meditating more on God's Word. I am less sick (I am on a different level) even the coughs are not as bad as before. They got fewer and fewer with maybe a little sniffle at times that only last for a minute or two.

We have to be careful about what we say when waiting on sickly and elderly people. God hears our words. Do some of you remember saying these following words? "I have to go home straight from work." "I am tired waiting on them." Or else, "I am getting up and down constantly all through the night." Maybe this one, "I have to travel long distances back and forth." "I am not able to get enough sleep." Here is a few more: "I cannot afford to care for them." "They are too heavy for me to lift." Just to name a few. God may take your burden away. He hears you!

Let us think on this for a moment. Our bodies are getting fatter and fatter. We are doing more evilness. We are breaking God's covenant more day by day by being hardheaded. We are making God angrier minute by minute. We are ungrateful and are getting more selfish. We have gotten very unforgiving. We are not using our common sense and getting denser by the minute. We have forgotten who our Provider is. So tell me now, why do we think we should get God's blessings. Do not forget that there is a penalty to pay for being rebellious. Yes, there will be tribulations. Not only for you, but they will also be handed down from generation to generation. We can encounter illnesses from diseases from not being obedient to God's Commandments and agreements. If you do not believe being obedient is serious business, just think about the sickness of Jehoram. He was struck with a terminal disease for being disobedient. We need to wake up God's sheep. Do you really want to be sick by not following God's Commandments or be sick-free for obeying them? Now you decide!

Chapter 9

NO FORMS OF INFIDELITY

Many times when we talk about infidelity, we bring up the different men in the Bible that had numerous extramarital affairs in order to make a point. Some of the men of today often compare themselves to them. They have stated that their affairs do not come even close to the numerous mistresses that Solomon and David had. Of course, you know that some of the women counteracted by stating that those affairs also brought on big trouble for them. What it all boils down to is that God does not want us to have any forms of infidelity rather it is texting, computer gazing, coveting, etc. with anyone else besides your spouse. Some of you might be saying right now that looking does not hurt. If so, you need to reconsider it. Do not forget that David's infidelity all started out of just looking.

Let's reflect a little more on the Biblical period. If you think about it for a moment, most of the time back then, when married men had extramarital affairs, he had already gotten his wife's approval beforehand. It was not behind her back. She complied mostly because she wanted kids so bad and because her husband had to procreate children with the other woman. However, the husband could adequately support them all. Now go ahead and think about this for a moment, how many spouses of today would let his or her spouse marry another spouse? You are right, not that many. Even when Jacob was tricked by getting multiple wives, it proved you would love one more than you would the other. It showed how hard it was for a man to love two women whole-heartedly. So, do not try this at home (Ha...Ha!!)

When you are in a marriage, you should be at a point where you would not want to desire another person.

You Want to Stop Sinning...Stop

The spouse that you choose will be as if you just won the grand prize. The prize was a meal at a great buffet restaurant for life. The spouse represents the meal. The spouse is the full meal deal, which is more than just an appetizer, salad, or entrée. Now, right after you had eaten and gotten full at the buffet, your friends call and asked you to meet them at another restaurant to talk about something important. Your friends hand you a menu. The menu items at the restaurant should not be appealing to you. It does not matter how good it looks or even if you were at your favorite restaurant. You do not want anything else to eat. You had gotten full at the buffet, which symbolized your spouse and that's all the meal you should need.

Let me take a guess now. You may be one of the ones that felt you did not get full at the buffet. The foods on the menu were too tempting for you. You may go ahead and order off the menu. Let me go ahead and disclose a little something to you. Stepping into a marriage is not for you until you have made some vital changes in your life, especially with God. God wants us to be satisfied with the full meal deal, the spouse He has given us!

God commanded us not to do any type of adulterous act, if so, we will be brought to ruin. This means that nothing great would come out of cheating. That's why not only our body should be for our spouse only, but our heart and mind should be theirs too, and we should be as one. We should be clear of any type of infidelity action whether looking on the computer, phone texting, watching nonstop the person walking down the row of the isle. *"Ye have heard that it was said by them of old time, THOU SHALT NOT COMMIT ADULTERY: But I say unto you, That whosoever looketh on a woman to lust after her hath committed adultery with her already in his heart"* *(Matthew 5:27-28).* Okay God's sheep, this forbidden act is nothing new. We often times want the blessing God has given to others instead of wanting our own blessing from

God. We should stop calling or emailing anyone else that is not our spouse 50 times a day or texting them 100 times a day. No, that person is not your friend. If so, they would not encourage it. Your spouse is waiting to hear from you too, now call and text him or her. You know the one who you were too busy and did not have time to contact today. We have to learn how to do like Joseph did and run. We have to escape from the wickedness. You still wonder why your marriage is not working. Who is your mind on? Do you not think that your spouse actually knows when someone else is clogging up your mind? News flash, they know that you are not giving them your all. God had that spouse tailor-made just for you and no other one would fit you so perfectly, so stop two-timing on your spouse. Parallel to God wanting us to have only one God, He means for us to have only one spouse. He does not want anything or anyone to hinder us for loving our spouse with all our heart. Being faithful and honest to our spouse starts first by being faithful to God. This is where some practices of faithfulness should have already been established.

Since our body is a temple, it should be holy. We have to watch what we do to and with our body. Can you just hear us: "He or she would not know." "It is just a movie." "It's not in real life, only on the internet." "It's not the same as sex." "I was just having fun." "He or she treated me wrong." "He or she was not spending enough time with me." "He or she was ignoring me." "He or she did it, so I can do it too." "He or she has gotten older." "He or she is not fun anymore." "He or she has changed." "I do not love him or her anymore." Nah, you had not fallen out of love; you fell out of commitment. If you had stayed committed, you would have found that love was still there. Yes, all of those mentioned above were reasons, but not excuses. Remember God's Word that we should be able to handle all those loads of temptations that will come our way, including lusting.

You Want to Stop Sinning...Stop

You and your spouse should be as one individual and no one should come between you and your spouse. Why do you think in the Bible it stated that you have found a good thing? We often sometimes hear that the thrill has vanished, the love stopped, or that they are no longer in love with them anymore. Are you sure that it was not all about lusting instead of love? Lusting is like a turn on and off switch. Is love that simple that you can turn on and off and now it's gone? What about your love for God, did you turn your love switch on and off for Him too? That's why we should be led by the spirit in our lives to help incorporate love and humbleness. Do you know exactly what characteristics that you should look for in a spouse? Were they all the right characteristics that God would have wanted for you or were they all about your own physical desires?

God has great plans for us. If you keep your faith in God, you will see that God blesses the ones that stand up to their temptations. Do not worry if you do not have a spouse. God will find you a wife or husband. He has one in store just for you. If not, then the one that you may quickly choose will last for just a short time. However, if you are patience, the ones that God put together will last a lifetime. No, God does not tempt us. Remember, all temptations that we have come from our own desires, so do not put it on our mind or think even about it. It all depends on what we want in our own hearts then the next thing that happens is that we start reacting to it. The devil will give out smoke signals trying to get in, but we cannot let him in. The devil knows exactly what we like and how to set it up for us in a nice pretty bow, and it will be all gift-wrapped for us. Blessed are those ones that can resist the temptation.

Most of the time when an individual cheats in a relationship they are really trying to find their identity. They do not know what they want. They are unstable and not able to commit to one individual. Those individuals have to learn also how to control their bodies. Yes, this does require practice. That's why all of this should take place before getting married and not vice versa.

My Sacrifice: *You have to have the right mindset. The mindset is an important factor of a non-adulterous marriage. I had already decided in my mind that I was going to be faithful. These thoughts have to be made beforehand which prepared me for any temptation that came across my way. Believe me, it will come your way.*

In order to help me deal with temptation and to ensure that I was doing what was right in God's eyes; the repetition of being faithful in my single life carried me over into my marriage. You are at a big disadvantage if you start being faithful once you get marry and thinking that now I will be faithful, but had not been at all faithful in any prior relationships. You may think, now this is the one (yeah, right).

Our body should be kept clean from the inside, outside, top, and bottom. I had to learn to keep my temple uncontaminated from any type of outside sources. I had to be able to abstain from many things and keep full control of my body at all times in every situation. God has given us everything that we need in order for our body to function. If we were not born with it then evidently we can do without it. I knew that I had to protect myself from any kind of sexual wickedness rather on the computer, television, or chatting on the telephone. No, it was not easy, but that is what I had to do and I was eager to do it; by keeping my faith in God, and asking God to remove any type of that taste from my mouth. You cannot do anything without Him and you have to meditate on God's Word day in and day out.

Here is a quick note for the single folks that may be messing around with a married person: Do not allow a married person give you a little piece of money and then be ready to sell your soul, I hear what you're saying. I was not married. It was not my problem. You need to make some immediately changes in your life in order for you to avoid this temptation. The devil will get even busier with you. One of the changes that you need to make is the way that you watch television. Depending on the scene, you have to change the channel, vacate the room, or close your eyes. You have to pray often in the name of Jesus to rebuke that temptation from you and ask God to help you climb that mountain (yes, even relating to things in your dreams). Hopefully, my married readers were taking some notes too.

It is a good thing that we are not dealing with adulterous act like they did back in the Israelites days. If so, both parties would be dead. The Israelites made sure that they put away this type of wickedness from around them and were not going to condone any of it.

Extramarital relationships should not be permitted, and that's with an exclamation mark. There should be no challenges to see how many relationships we can accomplish or how many feathers we can put in our hats. We should be honest and truthful in our relationships at all times; if not, we are asking for a disastrous marriage. Marriage is a serious step and it should not be taken likely. We should never want to mislead or hurt our spouse, which should be like doing it to ourselves since we are as one. So let's stop mistreating our spouse and thinking we are too good for them. Be the way God wants us to be as inseparable and love our spouse as we love God, and putting no others before them.

Chapter 10

NO TAKING OF OTHERS' PROPERTIES

This particular Commandment entails many categories from embezzlement, shoplifting, robbery, burglary, and the list keeps going on-and-on. Nevertheless, we cannot forget the ones that are normally swept under the rug like claiming an exemption, deduction, or receiving a check that you were not entitled. Yes, you are not only stealing from the system, but from others too. God commanded us not to steal or take anyone's properties. Even if we try to soften it up, it does not matter. Regardless of how many ways you want to look at it, toss it around, or say it; you are taking properties that belong to someone else. Even if you found it, it is still not yours to keep. No, it is not a gift from God. You have to give it back and let that person give it to you if they want. Then, you can say God wanted you to have it.

Sure, I cannot forget about you others too. Of course, you are the clever ones. The ones who say, "I will pay it back" or "bring it back tomorrow." Other excuses may be someone has taken mine or now it is only fair or it was not really considered their property, it was for anybody. We have to stop giving excuses to take other properties.

We have to have the faith that God will provide. He will always come through at the right time for us. God will not let us down. He will do as He did for Abraham and always will have a ram in the bush for us.

Not only do we steal, but most of the time we are also too greedy in order to get more money on top of money. Sometimes we steal just to get back at someone that did us wrong. We decide to pay him or her back and take something from him or her. We also take things that we really do not need just for bragging rights. We are too materialistic. When we take things it shows exactly where our heart is, wrapped around our money and what we possess. God does not even want us to work ourselves to death just to get plenty of money to live wastefully. He does not want anything to keep us from giving Him our whole heart.

My Sacrifice: *I had to make a decision long time ago when I was younger not to take something that did not belong to me. I can recall when I was coming from practice one day that one of my teammates went into a neighborhood store. Yes, you can say that I was following the crowd. It was not because I needed to, but just doing what someone else was doing. We went into the store. My friend stole a snack cake, so I stole one too. I knew it was wrong, but I did it anyway. It was not as if I was hungry. Once I did, I did not feel right about it. It was something in my conscience that kept telling me that it was not right. I believe God was heavy on my heart.*

Later on, we continued to go to that same store. My friend continued to misbehave. I continued to do what was right. I believed something came over my friend because my friend discontinued her misbehavior. I believe God worked on my friend too. Now before you start laughing, put that pen down. It is not yours. Of course, you were just borrowing it. Or it may be something minimal as taking food off someone's plate without his or her permission. The fact remains that we should not keep doing it. We do not want that type of spirit around. I was determined back then that I would never again take someone else's property.

When we steal, we are actually implying that we do not have confidence in God to provide for us. We have to be patient. Just remember, as I mentioned earlier, God will always have a ram in the bush for us. God is always on time, every time. God wants us to work for what we need so that we do not have to resort to stealing. *"Let him that stole steal no more: but rather let him labour, working with his hands the thing which is good, that he may have to give to him that needth" (Ephesians 4:28).* By us being employed, we will have resources to provide for our needs and then some resources to help others. This will prevent them for having to steal just to put a roof over their heads, clothes on their backs, or even food on their tables. We will serve as a great role model and a prime example of showing them how it should be done. When God bless us, it is not only for our enjoyment, but also for us to be a blessing and help someone else. This includes those beyond our immediate family members. When we do, God will bless us even more in whatever we do.

We say what God has for us is for us then why are we conniving, stealing, cheating, lying, scheming, backstabbing, etc. On the other hand, we should not have to bamboozle anyone. Wherever our mind and our money is that's where our true love is. That is why we have become more selfish and why we're trying to beat money out of others without earning the money. God knows where our heart is. He knows what we're trying to please more than Him. We definitely do not want the individuals that we have scammed to pray out to God regarding our selfish activities.

Most of us probably have stolen something in our lifetime. How about when you did not pay someone or some company back, and you know that you owe them. Yes, that's stealing! Whether it was a pen or pencil, at school or at work, candy, grapes, nuts in grocery store, or money out of spouse's or parent's purse. For others it may have been change under the couch or under a car seat. If we did not put it there, we know who it might be. It did not have our name on it. The list can go on-and-on. Yes, it maybe it was something simple, but it was not yours.

God loves us and will provide and bless us with what we need. We have to keep our faith in Him and believe that He will not let us go without our necessities. When most of us steal it is not out of need but more out of greed. We have to pray to our Father and He will take care of us because He knows what we need. God asked us to put Him first, and all the other things will be provided for us. God will give us all we need and we do not have to steal or swindle anyone or any company out of anything. Just keep our faith in God and He will provide!

Chapter 11

DO NOT LIE

Yes, you have read the name of the title of this chapter correctly. This chapter does pertain to lying. We should not tell a lie, whether it's a small one or a big one. I remember mom telling me when I was younger; your so-called friends are not your friends, just your associate. They are not only mischievous, but they are also dishonest. They grin in your face and throw rocks behind your back. God commanded us not to be a partaker of being dishonest by being a liar. He wants us to be truthful in all things that we do or say. We should be the same way towards Him.

Normally, when we start lying it will lead to slandering next. We often lie and slander someone's name because we are jealous or want revenge in order to cause him or her harm. Moses' sister and brother gossiped about him marrying an Ethiopian woman. Do you not remember what happened to Miriam? She got a skin disease. That is why you should not slander anyone, especially since you do not know who has a close relationship with God. It is a disgrace to God when we always start dissension among each other. We act as if we have to be starting up something. Just like they slandered Jesus although He kept telling them that He came in God the Father's name.

My mom use to say some people will tell a lie when the truth is just as good. She stated they could have just told the truth. There would be no cause to make up a story to tell. The truth was just a good of an explanation as the lie. The reason for this is because they had become orbital liars, it had become habit forming for them. They make up a fabricated story before even realizing they had done it. It had become natural to them. Our words used to mean something. A person would not say it if he or she did not mean it and were not going to follow it through. Today words are just a lot of noise making.

We need to stop telling lies because it will eventually catch up with us, it is just the matter of when. Do you not realize in order to speak negative about someone you must be thinking about him or her and he or she must be on your mind? We should always want to ensure that when we speak about someone we are speaking the truth and something good. We should always be willing to try to find a way to encourage everyone. Since we want to talk about someone, then let's always speak positive about the person.

When we tell a lie on someone it is like telling a lie on our own ourselves because we are all as one whether we realize it or not. Of course, we would not want to lie on ourselves. *"Wherefore putting away lying, SPEAK EVERY MAN TRUTH WITH HIS NEIGHBOUR: for we are members one of another" (Ephesians 4:25).* Do not be jealous of anyone and start boasting evil lies about him or her. Even if we say we were just joking, we are still telling lies. This is where it hit home for me.

My Sacrifice: *I was caught up being a jokester. I had to stop and catch myself from joking that way. My joking would sometimes contain lies and short stories that I made up just to get a laugh. I loved to see a smile on someone's face, but, it should not be made in that way. Yes, I had to come clean with my readers on this one.*

It is ironic though because my son had to get me straight on this particular Commandment. My son told me that it did not matter even it is a joke, a lie is still being told. It is something when your son had to call you out to the front and correct you. It was so true. I was telling what some might say, a "little lie." I had to stop doing it. Even though, I was just kidding around. I stopped joking with lies. I loved to smile and continually tried to get others to smile too. Do not get me wrong. There is

60

nothing wrong with smiling (shows how great our God is), but what was wrong was the false content of the jokes that I was using.

I have struggled with this commandment even when writing this book. I have had a few episodes where I continued to joke with a made up lie to get a laugh. I had to pray dearly, asking God for guidance and assistance to put a stop to it. I can see the changes in me. I guess you can say, I had to start judging myself.

Some may try to down play it and say, "Oh it's nothing wrong with that." If so, you are not getting it. You should not want that lying spirit on you because later it becomes habit forming. Then instead of being a joke you start lying just about anything. You have to remember, lying starts out small then it gets bigger and deeper. You start being dishonest with individuals just to make a dollar. You would be gipping individuals for items, services, etc. God wants us to be fair and have good ethics. He does not want us to deceive anyone but He wants us to do what's right. We have to start worshiping God by being real, with no gimmicks.

Do not lie on or about others. It is about doing what's right. If you told that lie, you need to confess your wrongdoing to each other and pray for one another. Not only does it put peace in your heart, but it also you will gain much by yielding a friend. Remember, your tongue that you use is powerful, and can be harmful or helpful. Be careful not to use it to be deceitful or use it to be envious of someone. That includes judging unfairly or lying just to make a profit. In a competition we don't want to win by lying and beating someone at any cause.

We should not have animosities or deceitfulness, towards each other even with in our own family members. We don't want to deceive our own brothers, sisters, dads, or moms, like Jacob (a.k.a. Israel) deceived His dad for birthrights. Later, it caught up with him and he got deceived himself by marrying the wrong sister.

We need to stay away from this evil lying spirit. As mentioned earlier, moms knew best. She knew if we hung out with individuals that were doing bad and evil things that it would soon lead us down that same road. It was not that she did not trust us. It was because being around different types of evil spirits could end up causing them to jump from one individual to another. The same way with the lying spirit, it can go from one person to another person. Now you may be wondering why your child tells lies and where it came from and how it got started (Hint…look around your home).

Even in our court system, it is hard to distinguish if some is really lying or not. It may have been the other person just had a better representation to plead his or her case. If you are not a fast or smooth talker, then you may miss discovering that someone has just told you a fib. This is how many kids or even adults have gotten into a lot of trouble and could not get out because of not being a fast or smooth talker. Later on, they were found innocent. Individuals would ask them why didn't you say anything. It may have been because you were not paying close attention when others were less outspoken. In the end, God really knows who is really lying or telling the truth.

When someone comes across your mind that has done you wrong, instead of gossiping about them and taking a chance, you may perish on lies that you may have added to the conversation. Why not pray for them instead by handing it over to God? You finish up with "in Jesus' name." Since Jesus' name is so powerful it is best to say, "thank you Jesus" and see how fast that individual leaves your mind. If anything is on your mind and you want to get it off quickly just say, "thank you Jesus," and it will get off your mind immediately.

You Want to Stop Sinning...Stop

When you tell a lie on someone that same lie you told could come back fully blazing on you. If you think lying is not a serious matter, think about Ananias when he lied and kept some of the money from the sale of his own land. He died right there on the spot.

Being dishonest can come in many forms. You can not only be telling a fib, but you could be lying about measurements, different weight products, pyramid schemes, on your assessments, or beating others out of their money. Yes, it could be on anything that tries to get financial gain dishonestly. Yes, it could be investment swindles too. You could also be charging higher prices instead of what is actually due. If we do these things, our days on this earth may be cut short. We should be good to everyone. We should not lie, whether so-called little lies or big lies; not even, if we are just telling a little story just for a joke or two. We have to stop lying and be honest with each other, which in return will mean we're being honest with ourselves.

Chapter 12

DO NOT ENVY

How many times have we said, "I wish I had all the money he or she has? If I did, I would know what to do with it." Okay, maybe you did not say that one. Maybe you stated, "If I had a house like that one I would know how to take care of it." Now when you said those things it was not to say it in admiration, but more in indignation. We envy what they have and we want it. We want it more because somebody else has it.

We have to be carefully not to get in the mode of desiring or wanting something so bad because someone else has it. Yes, we should not to crave, cry for, wish for, grumble, complain, whine, moan, or long for someone else's things or even their spouse. God commanded us not to covet what others have and that includes their clothes, spouse, money, home, boyfriend, girlfriend, car, jewelry, etc. That also includes desiring other people's jobs. There is no need to because God already has a job waiting just for us. He knows what's best for us because He made us. What God has for us is always better than what we could ever wish for. Besides, we do not know what the other person went through to get what they got. If so, would we really want their grief too?

Being envious of someone comes mostly from jealousy, hating, being selfish, materialistic, or being just down right greedy. Most of the time, we actually do not need their things or really care for their spouse that they have. We just do not want to see them with it or with him or her. The Bible tells us: *"Envyings, murders, drunkenness, revellings, and such like: of the which I tell you before, as I have also told you in time past, that they which do such things shall not inherit the kingdom of God" (Galatians 5:21).* By exploiting "hater raid," will not get us into Heaven. There is no need to be envy or hating on anyone for what they have. God has plenty for all of us. There is enough to go around.

Sometimes we want to complain and whisper things under our breath. Do we not know that God hears us? I guess you may wonder why you do not have what they have. It is mainly because of being ungrateful for what you do have. We have to stop passing rumors and gossiping about others. All of this grumbling and complaining will not make us get anything any quicker. It just may be what is delaying what we got coming. We need to stop picking holes at someone and taking them apart. Therefore, stop finding fault and criticizing why someone has it and we do not have it. We are not actually criticizing them, but really criticizing God. He is the one that can change a scenario.

We have to be thankful for what God has given us. We have to be of good courage. God does not want to hear our negative statements. We definitely do not want to be like the Israelites in the wilderness by being ungrateful for what God had given us. Some of them died of a plague because they caused the rest of the Israelites to complain to God.

Most of the times envy starts out wanting what others have and then it leads to hatred. Then the next thing we do is try to take it by stealing. What I am referring to is the cheating, carjacking, scamming, and embezzlement. When we covet anything that belongs to someone else, such as his or her money, it shows the lack of our trust and faith in God and that He has not given us enough to be able to live on. Most of the time when we covet something it is not what we need it is what we want. In most instances, we are just being greedy.

Do you wonder why so many of us get headaches trying to get rich? We work all hours of the day and night, wanting what someone else has. We should be more concerned with asking God to show us how to love one another and how to receive eternal life, not how to get rich quick. We should ask God for guidance and then follow His directions.

While we are envying what someone else has, we had better be careful what we pray for because we might just get it. Then we will realize it is not what we really wanted. God got something better for us, and it is personalized just for us. It is like our own monogram shirt. No other person can wear it, but you. It was designed for you only. Instead of being obsessed over what someone has and wanting to be like him or her, try to be patient and wait for God to give us what He has in store for us.

My Sacrifice: *I had to take myself out of the equation and be a little less selfish. I began by being all about God. I had to be careful about what I asked of God. I had to change the way that I prayed. Of course, who wouldn't want fine things like others have such as: homes, cars, or a great spouse? Regardless, we should stop looking on the outside inward. We have to stop watching over the fence and struggling to be like the Andersons. I decided that I wanted what God has for me. I knew whatever I asked for I would receive, if I put God first. I did not care what others said I should have. I wanted my own. I started being more appreciative and grateful of what God had already given me. I had to learn to be more attentive and listen to what God wanted for me. When I did, God gave me all that I needed and then some.*

We have to give God thanks for everything we have and stop our grumbling. God has provided us with food on our table, clothes on our backs, and roofs over our heads. By despising others because they have a new car or have gotten married and we haven't doesn't get us any closer to having what they have. We need to stop provoking God, so that we do not end up dying because of our own desires.

You Want to Stop Sinning...Stop

Do not forget, God loves us all, the poor as well as the rich. If we want to get rich in something, wish not to be rich in money, but ask God to give us richness in love, faith, and health. In addition, stop looking back on what you have had or should have had, you might end up like Lot's wife. Be content on what you do have. God has our back, sides, and front. He will take care of us and we will not be in need for anything.

Let's stop the cycle of hating on each other and start praying for one another. If someone comes across your mind, pray for him or her. If someone succeeds, just be glad for him or her. God will not only give us an increase, but will give us even more; and not only to us, but also to our children. Just believe whatever your situation is, good or bad, God will provide whatever you need. God is always there for us no matter how it appears.

Even though this particular Commandment may have been the last one given to Moses, the number ten (that we should not covet) but it does not make it less of importance. The Lord will provide for us. We should only have to ask. He will give to us. God will provide us everything within His plan for us. We should want what God puts our name on. I do not want it if my name is not inscribed on it by God!

God commanded us that we should not wish for what other people have. We should be thankful for all the things God has given us. The majority of the time even jealousy can start by coveting what someone else has. When we covet, it may lead to stealing, and then lying about it just to get it (disobeying more of God's Laws). Do not forget about Achan who kept the unadvised things of gold, silver, and garments of his opponent Jericho. He had hidden them in his tent because of being envious and badly wanting what someone else had. To show you that we should not covet his whole family was killed and burnt with all of those possessions. He had brought not only a curse on himself, but on his whole family as well. Do not envy others as the devil envies God. God will give us what we need. He knows what things we have lack of and what we need. We might want a car, but we may need a house to live in more. He knows which one and in what order to give them to us. Therefore, keep riding that bus. If we are patient there may be a car already lined up for someone to give it to us and then we will not have any monthly payments.

God will give us all that we need to survive in this world. We are all uniquely made and have different needs and should have different desires. God has already personalized what He has in store just for us. There is no need to envy and hate on others. We should be thankful for all the things God has given us and just be ourselves. If we all placed God first before all others and all things, we could not even imagine all the types of blessings we would receive.

Chapter 13

LOVE IS VITAL

All of the Commandments are linked into this one specific prerequisite, love. This is the most vital criterion given to us. Jesus commanded us to love. We need to try and learn the actual real true meaning of love. It is started first by loving God with everything we have inside of us. There is no one and nothing that should ever come before God. Yes, not even our spouse, parents, kids, friends, our money, or our electronics. Another meaning of that greatest Commandment is that we should love others the same way we love ourselves. Okay, I hear you wise guys! You may be thinking how about if you do not love yourself. You are reading this book, so you must do (me being another wise one too) love yourself.

The Pharisees had tried to tempt Jesus by asking which one of the Commandments were the greatest of the law. *"Jesus said unto him, THOU SHALT LOVE THE LORD THY GOD WITH ALL THY HEART, AND WITH ALL THY SOUL, AND WITH ALL THY MIND. This is the first and great commandment. And the second is like unto it, THOU SHALT LOVE THY NEIGHBOUR AS THYSELF" (Matthew 22:37-39).* You can also see in those above verses that love is the main piece of the puzzle. It is the common dominator in those Laws. Love is the most powerful tool to utilize.

Jesus had put it all in a simplified version for us. He gave us the full picture of what God is asking us to do by showing us about love. If you take time to marinate on it for a moment, love is such a wonderful thing that it sums up the first four of God's Ten Commandments together for us. If we love God with all our hearts, we would not have any other gods before Him. We would not want to create any type of graven image. In addition, if we truly love God we definitely would not be saying His name in vain. We would also want to keep the Sabbath day holy and get some rest as God requested us to do. Go ahead and continue marinating a little bit more on the second greatest Commandment. If we love everyone like we love ourselves, we would not want to harm them in any kind of way and would treat them with respect. By doing this, we would first love our parents and obey them. Of course, we would not want to kill anyone. We would be faithful to our spouse. We would not want to steal from anyone. Neither would we want to tell lies on any one. We definitely would not desire anything someone else has.

Since we know that love is the greatest Commandment of all, please tell me why this is not the number one subject taught in our household, at our school, or even to our congregation? Could it be because love is too simple of a topic? Or else, is it because everyone should know what love is? In any case, we might want to rethink this. Are we still wondering why there is a lot of wickedness happening in this world? It might be because we r-e-a-l-l-y do not know the true meaning of love. One thing that identifies true love is sacrifice.

After I started looking back at all the sacrifices that I have made, there was no sacrifice that I have made could compare or was more vital than this particular one. No, not one of my sacrifices could even compare or come close to it. The one that I am thinking about was the best sacrifice of all time. Could anyone's sacrifice put a hand on this one? I don't think so. This sacrifice was when God sacrificed His Son, Jesus Christ for us. He did this for us so that we could have eternal life. No one will ever sacrifice better than Jesus dying for our sins. God loved us so much that He gave us His Son. When God gave His Son, it showed us that He would give us anything. So why are we not giving God our best? Let me go ahead and ask this question in another way. Why are we still giving God our leftovers?

By now this should explain better the reason behind why I wanted to make sacrifices to God. Because He has given you and me so much. I thought about what sacrifices I could possibly make that would make God more proud of me? Therefore, I came up with those few that I had mentioned earlier in this book. I knew that making those sacrifices were going to be great challenges for me. Nevertheless, it did not matter to me because God has given me life.

Some may be thinking that you always sacrifice something to the Lord. We need to just make certain that it was not our last night's leftovers. In some instances when the sacrifice was made there was something left over to give, or there was not enough time left in the day when you decided to make a sacrifice and it was in a rush and not thought through properly.

We show our true love for God by demonstrating to God that we can keep His Commandments. God gave us these Commandments and agreements. Do you think God would have given them to us if they were too hard for us to do? It is just like medicine that does not taste good; it is not hard to take, just unpleasant for us to swallow. It is the same with the Commandments. It is not hard to do, it is just a hard pill to swallow when we do not want to do it. We have to be conscientious about what we are doing. We have to start judging and chastising ourselves. The commandments and agreements will not be hard for us to keep if we just put God first. God has to be "numero uno" in our life. We cannot do it without Him. We will struggle with it, as many of us are doing right now. Let me make this little plain; we cannot do anything without God.

We have to come in unity as God's people and begin working together as one. We have to treat each other right and love everyone. We have to ask God for guidance and ask Him to take any hardness in our heart from us. Do you think that maybe Jesus gave us these two main Commandments because He knew we could not do any of the other Commandments if hatred stayed in our heart? When we really love God or someone we would do anything for them, and we would not want to harm them in any kind of way. We should not let anything separate us from loving the one and only God, not even the devil. We should believe that Jesus Christ is God's Son. As well as believe that love is the main trait that we should all incorporate in our lives, more importantly than faith and hope.

Once we have the knowledge of God's love for us and believe that He sent His son to die for our sins. We cannot keep practicing wrongdoing over and over again. We have to change our ways. God love us more than we could ever imagine. He allowed His son to die for something that He did not do, just for us. This in itself should show us why love is the greatest Commandment of the Law. Even though we do not have to do it, but just out of love, we should all want to make some type of sacrifice daily to God with all of our heart. That is right. We should go out our way to get a smile on God's face even when we are feeling down and out ourselves. Our relationship with God should be similar to a marriage. We should try to love Him as much as He loves us.

Think about it, if everyone put others first for a change. Right before we did something or said something love would help us think about how it would affect others. God's sheep, we need to wake up now! We have to love others regardless of what they have done to us. In addition, we have to help others in spite of our own situation no matter what may be going on in our lives. We have to find a way to make it work for the both of us.

Love says it all and that's why it is vitally tied into all the Commandments. If you are looking for a solution to the root of all of your problems that you are facing in this world, love is the key. Yes, it is the antidote. If we first start by loving God, then each other, it would give us a better grip on things that are happening in our lives. We should always love each other with all our ability. Once you have utilized love, you will see how easy it is to forget about all that other mumbo-jumbo stuff. God is love. When God permitted His Son to die for us, it demonstrated to us that He was all about love. That's why we should be eager to make a daily sacrifice to God, to show our love for Him. Of course, if we really do love God, it would be reflected in our daily interactions. If everything that we did was out of love, imagine how wonderful this world would be.

Chapter 14

DESIRE TO STOP SINNING

I know if you are reading this book merely by accident or on purpose, you want to stop sinning. That is good! It all starts with these two words "desire and stop." You have to have the desire to want to stop. It is comparable to when you are driving a car when you come to a stop sign, you want to stop and of course, you did not keep going when you saw the sign. That showed evidence that you had the desire and the capability to stop and you had the perfective meaning of it. In addition, you already know how to be obedient when you are in the vicinity of a cop. You immediately slow down to be cautious whether you were speeding or not. You are giving him the honor right there and then. We should be displaying the same concept for God when we sin, because God is everywhere and He sees everything. We should be conscientious enough to stop our evil ways right there and then and give Him the honor. We know how to obey city and state laws, now how about us start having the desire to obey God's laws.

Okay, for those that do not drive, you thought that I was going to leave you out? You do go to sleep at night, right, even if it is for a minute or just a second (Ha!! Ha!!). Once again, you had to stop what you were doing in order to go to sleep. You had the desire and were able to display your stopping ability. Of course, you got it so down packed now that you are able to stop your activities in order to sleep every night.

God is the one that created us, and who knows us better as to what we are capable of doing. He knows all our abilities. Therefore, if we disobey one of God's Commandments, it is as if we have disobeyed them all. No one is flawless. We have to ask God for guidance. We have to decide whether we want the blessings or the cursings that are instore for us. If we obey God's Commandments, the curses would then be put on our haters instead of us. The devil would go on to his next victim once he sees that you are all about God's business. And do not give him a reason to come back to you either!

God gave us only ten things to follow. If God had given us too much at one time to do or comprehend it would have blown our minds. It would have overwhelmed us. The deeper your relationship with God the more you will understand what God is requiring all of us to do. That's why it is important to put time in with God. You will be amazed what you could abstain from doing. God did not give us Commandments that we could not obey or was unachievable. If we think that we cannot obey them then we are already beaten. Yes, that's right, the devil got us whipped. We cannot let the devil get the best of us. So do not wait for something tragic to happen to get you to stop sinning. There is no better time than right now.

We need to stop wandering around countless years in the wilderness. By this I mean doing whatever we want, and then keep going in circles by doing it over and over again. God ensured that most of the original crewmembers that came out of Egypt had died off completely before entering the Promise Land. This was because of their disobedience by not following God's Commandments. We do not have to act also as if we were as the Israelites. We do not want to die before our time by being disobedient. We do not have to hurry our life away!

Stop saying the devil made you do it! We have to take accountability for our own actions. We still did not have to do it. Now tell me, who do you think really are our enemies? Correct, we are our own worst enemies. If you were tempted then that's why you did it. Since we know we will be tempted we must have confidence that there will be a way out from giving in to that temptation. *"There hath no temptation taken you but such as is common to man: but God is faithful, who will not suffer you to be tempted above that ye are able; but will with the temptation also make a way to escape, that ye may be able to bear it" (1 Corinthians 10:13).* We are all going to be tempted to do evil things. That's nothing new. God is there for us and we can count on Him. God will always give us a way out of no way for us to handle that sin which may come across our path. We have to decide if we are the devil's children or God's children. If you are the devil's children, then do what the devil wants you to do, which is evil. However, if you are God's children, then do what God wants you to do, which is good.

We have to learn how to conquer ourselves. God is always loyal and will be there for us. He will be there to help us to stop the desires of our hearts in wanting to do what's wrong. How we conquer ourselves is by controlling our body and our minds. We should not let the devil take control of us. Things are going to happen in our lives. We have to make the very best of the situation and handle it God's way. We have to put our trust in God and let Him be our guide. If Jesus cannot do anything without God, why do we think we can? We need God's grace and strength to help us to be obedient to His Commandments. We have been handling our temptations by ourselves far too long on our own. God will not let the evilness get the best of us. God will deliver us. We have to listen to Him.

I mentioned before, God gives us a way out from doing wickedness. We have to decide if we want to take part in it, or if we want to encounter the evil situation. Some of you may be saying right now, "When did I get a way out?" You remember when you were single or married and you attempted to date two people at a time. There was a person that you may have been lusting after and finally that person no longer worked with you and moved out of your area, or lost interest in you. Yet, you still decided to pursue them anyway. Listen...Listen!!! God moved that person out of your reach and away from you for or a reason. God gave you a way out. But you did not take the escape plan.

In addition, we have to stop using our mouth and tongue to talk negative about each other but instead use our tongue to be like fire for God. Our words should also keep spreading like wildfire. Not even water or anything, or no one should be able to stop us. We should use our words to feed God's sheep by informing them to keep God's Commandments, and to stop sinning. We have to let them know that if they keep God's Laws that they are helping to keep their souls. Let them also know that if they keep sinning it will only lead to death. We have to stop being selfish and loving ourselves more than we love God. We have to turn from our evil ways and any ways that may appear to others that we may be doing evil, and then repent and be baptized. You never know who may be watching your every move and thus hinder their progress. God wants all our souls. He does not want anyone to perish.

In some kind of form or fashion, we should be trying to recompense for what we have done wrong. We should immediately "confess" to God and "repent" of all the evil things we have done. We should always be trying to make it right with God. Our sins are forgiven not because of who we are, but because of who Jesus is and how great God is. We should not be falling into loving what the world has to offer us, but falling in love with what God has to offer us.

We are searching to find peace but cannot find any because of our sins. We will be punished to the extent of what we deserve. God will give us peace from our enemies if we do not endorse sin. We have to learn how to put God first and ask for His guidance. He will teach us how to control sin. Do not let sin control us. Therefore, do what is right and obey God's Commandments.

You Want to Stop Sinning...Stop

When we break God's Commandments, there will be numerous conflicts within our lives. Everything we do will only be in vain. God wants us to be privileged to all kinds of things, you just name it. He agreed to give it to us if it coincides with His plan for our lives. If we do not do what is right in God's eyes, by obeying His Laws and continue to do according to our own selfish made up laws, we will nerve ever get, nor be able to touch the surface of what God has planned for us. God said he would put it on our hearts to do what is right. There are no excuses to do what is wrong when we know to do better. Sin is the only thing that comes between God and us. Sin is waiting for a tag team partner. Do you really want to be it? Of course you do not!!!!

Moses had made an oath that there would be a blessing or a curse on the Ten Commandments. If we follow the Commandments, it is a blessing. If we do not obey the Commandments, it will be a curse to us. God's requirements are, for us is to honor Him, to obey His Commandments, to love Him, and to be a true servant. We need to walk in the Spirit and not give in to our flesh. We have to have faith to stop sinning and to make sure that we do what is right. It all starts with us first. Then next, we have to forgive others. We have to do the right thing in our hearts instead of doing what we want to do in our own minds. We have to stop that "do not care" attitude. We should care about the consequences of what will happen to us or what will happen to us when we die. There will be no peace of mind for us while we are still corrupt. We have to get on the right track and stop neglecting God's covenant. We are aware of the blessings that God will give us, but we still decide to do what we want to do in spite of what we know. There will be curses upon us as it was in the destruction of Admoh and Zeboim for their evil work. If we do not obey, there will be a fulfillment of all the curses that are mentioned in the Bible. There may also be ones we have not even heard of yet, and not only on us, but also on our future generations.

If we turn from our evil ways and obey God's Commandments, God will have compassion for us. We have to make that U-turn. God will turn the curses on us to our enemies. God gives us choices in our lives to do good or to do evil. To live or to die, we need to just obey God's Commandments and agreements so that our generations to come will prosper and receive blessings here on this earth. The price that we will pay for continuing to sin leads to death only. The price of doing right, by following God's ways is eternal life through Jesus Christ. We have to love God with our full heart and not be half-stepping. God is forever and there is no other gods. This is why Jesus best summed up the Commandments for us in two Commandments; that it is all about the love for God, and the love for one another.

Are you still wondering why some things still happen to us? Some of them are because of our own fault. Moses made sure the Israelites understood the consequences if the Commandments were not obeyed. God made a promise to our ancestors if His Commandments were met. Do you not think that these same things apply to us if we reject His Commandments? There will be disasters that will come upon us. We will be chastised for misbehaving. On the flipside, if we do obey what God commanded us there will be so many blessings that it will overwhelm us. It would be reflected in everything we do. Everyone would automatically know and see that we are blessed.

We need to thank God for His grace that we do not die as quickly as in the Israelites' days when we disobey His Commandments. Some sins back then were automatic dismissals. We would all have been dead on the spot. Yes, there was zero tolerance. Even now, we still have to obey them. If not, there will be consequences. Most of us are familiar with God stating that He would not destroy us all with a flood as previously done during Noah's days. I believe that is why today we are taking advantage of God's kindness. We are trying to see just how much we can get away with.

Once we are aware of the gospel of Jesus Christ, we do not have a license to keep on sinning just for the fun of it. We are now held more accountable. We cannot be like someone who keeps falling in a ditch and someone keeps pulling us out. We kept falling in on purpose just to get them to pull us out again because they were nice, and they had done it before. *"For if we sin wilfully after that we have received the knowledge of the truth, there remaineth no more sacrifice for sins" (Hebrews 10:26).* This verse does a good job with showing us that we cannot keep on sinning just because we can sin. In other words, we cannot sin at will. Even though, Jesus died for all our sins. He did not give us a ticket to keep sinning on purpose. He died, so we do not have to be sinful nature. Jesus had blessed us from sin. When we sin intentionally, we are throwing it in God's face and taking advantage of His generosity. Do you not know when we do then God sacrificing His Son for our sins is being made void by us? We annulled it when we deliberately kept sinning. Wake up God's sheep! Do we not realize what our final destination will be if we continue doing all this wickedness?

For those that have already decided, you are not ever going to obey God's Commandments. Here is something that I need to tell you. You will be chastised for being disobedient. It is going to appear to you as if you are standing still in one spot and cannot move. Every time you take two steps, you will feel that you are going back three steps. It will appear to you that you can never get ahead. There will be one whipping right after another. You would be continually going through this until you have repented and stopped being disobedient.

You Want to Stop Sinning...Stop

Therefore, right now at this moment let us stop making "199" excuses why we cannot stop intentional sinning. Yes, we can do anything, but it all starts by just asking God Almighty for guidance. Does not that word "anything" include sin too? God gives us the strength to overcome it through Jesus Christ. We have to take a deep look at ourselves and be willing and eager to take that initiative to want to change. Let's break this cycle now, and start waking up as God's sheep!

Yes, we have to turn away from those evil ways and repent. There is a place for you to go to help you get some remedies. That place is in the Bible. It has the answers and instructions on how to correct your behavior. God's Commandments are clear about what we should or should not be doing. If you do not quite understand what is requested of us, then ask God in prayer. It is a time for us to do right by God's standards, according to His ways, and not by doing things our own way or the way of someone else's selfish eyes.

The blessed are the ones that actually perform God's Words, not just hear and saying them. We all say that we will not let anyone misuse us. So, tell me why are we falling into the devil's hands and doing his dirty work for him? We should be performing God's good work. Look now in the mirror and tell me what do you see? Is there any one standing next to you pointing a gun to your head? If so, are they telling you to keep sinning and don't stop? I did not think so, but it might as well have been because you are heading in the same direction. By you intentionally sinning over and over again, it only leads to death. You are the only one that can make that choice as to whether you will continue to sin or put a stop it. Will you give in to your own desires and keep doing evil? Or else, will you repent and obey God's Commandments and agreements? The choice is yours. What choice will you make? You decide!

Chapter 15

WINDING UP

How familiar does this sound? If I were back in the days of Adam and Eve, I would not have bitten that fruit (a.k.a apple). I would have known better and obeyed God's directive. Is this not us? We say this every time we hear or read the story of Adam and Eve. However, each day, we are biting a fruit, but this time the difference is that we keep biting a rotten fruit. The frightening thing is, it appears that we like it. The metaphor for the fruit is sin, and that we keep biting into it over and over again. Therefore, we are just as bad as Adam and Eve. We are still not obeying God's directives. It's deja vu all over again. God gave us Ten Commandments to follow, but we are not following them.

Just like we teach our kids to tie their shoes, do multiplication tables, or to follow household rules, we should be teaching our kids the Ten Commandments all throughout the day (morning, noon, and night) in some kind of form or fashion. Yes, it should be that frequent. It should be planted so deep into their minds that they should never stop wanting to do what God requires of them. It should be part of their daily game plan. The Commandments will help maintain them, give them hope, and guide them by revealing what to do. The Commandments should also be hung somewhere in the house so that everyone may see them. We should also start from ground zero, teaching God's lambs on how to love one another. If love is not taught, we will soon find ourselves diminishing from the face of the earth, and our life and blessings will be cut short.

God has implanted in our hearts and our minds to do what's right. We should aim for perfection to be like our Father God. We have to listen to what He is telling us to do and then obey. *"But it shall come to pass, if thou will not hearken unto the voice of the Lord thy God, to observe to do all his commandments and his statutes which I command thee this day; that all these curses shall come upon thee, and overtake thee" (Deuteronomy 28:15):* God's Laws consist of blessings and cursings. We have to make a decision to do right instead of wrong. We need God's help and guidance. We cannot do anything without God, nor can we do anything without Jesus.

God does not want us to be dedicated to the devil or any gods. He does not want us to end up in h-e-l-l. We should be using all of our God given power to do what is right and being faithful to Him. One way we can show our faithfulness is by going to church. There should never be an excuse for us not to go to church. There may be reasons why you do not go, but never an excuse. I can recall when I was younger that going to church was not an option. I was faithful going to church every Sunday regardless of how tired I was from school, working a job, or just from hanging out on a Saturday night. I was there rain or shine. We have to all get back to being that devoted to honoring God.

We have to be careful of what we look at, think, and do. Even when we think that we have not done anything wrong we still need to be cautious. We say that we do not go to a psychic. At least that's what the majority of us would say. Yet, this psychic comes to us daily, just be careful. This particular one is on our television or on our phone predicting the weather for us for the next few days. Have you tried asking God, the controller, to see what the weather would be? I can tell you one thing, He will always be right!

We need to thank God for absolutely everything. Yes, even if we are in poverty. God will turn it all around for us. We have to keep our faith in Him. God will always give us what we need at the right time. Just like it took practice for us to do what was wrong, it takes practice for us to do what is right. We will get better with it like anything else, then later it will become natural to us. We would have formed a habit. As our parents and coaches use to say, "Keep doing it." We will get better at it. It will also show that our faith is working too.

The best way you can resist the devil is by praying and consistently reading your Bible. This will help keep you from falling into temptation as you take notes from Jesus. God's Words are so helpful with fighting against anything the devil may throw your way. It also shows that you have wisdom when you obey God's Commandments and use His Words. This type of wisdom we should be passing down from generation to generation. God's main objective is to save everyone.

The sacrifices that I made to God have manifested a change in me. I started viewing others in a more loving and caring way. I was giving people more of a benefit of a doubt. The sacrifices that I made also assisted me in being more in compliance with God's Commandments. It aided me on how to better discipline myself. Even Jonas learned a great lesson about being obedient. He began warning his enemies. God had kept giving his enemies chances after chances. If they would stop sinning, He would turn away from being angry with them. We, as God's sheep, cannot keep straddling with one leg on this side of the line trying to do right, and the other leg on the other side of the line doing what is wrong. We also definitely do not want to end up like the people in Gomorrah and Sodom. God could not find one God-fearing individual in order to save those cites.

As I mentioned before, we all have "sinned". That is a given. The word is used in the past tense, which means we do not have to keep doing it in the present tense. We use the wording that "we all have sinned" as an excuse to keep on sinning and we do not even try to stop. We do not have to utilize our so-called "sinning certificate" to keep on

You Want to Stop Sinning...Stop

sinning by keep murdering, lying, hurting, stealing, cheating, being disrespectful, heartless, etc. We need to repent and do better. This also doesn't mean that one person is better than the other person. We are all the same. Good is in our nature, do not let the evilness take it over. Sinning should be far in between and not something that we purposely do day in and day out.

We say that we love God, but how can we, when we do not keep His Commandments. God will be merciful to the ones that really love Him if they continue keeping His Commandments. It is just that simple. There is no other way around it. We have to do what God commanded us to do. It is now time to repent for all the evilness; not only for what we have done, but also for what others have also done. Remember that the sin that we do can follow us from generation to generation. We should ask for forgiveness for our ancestors for their wrongdoing as well as our own. We do not really want God to put the hammer on us according to our evil deeds. He will show us no pity if we do not stop our evil ways and repent.

We need to start teaching others to obey God's Commandments and Covenants. Just like Moses taught the Israelites about God's Laws. Jesus came to save us by teaching us love and to do good rather than evil. He did not come to destroy us or to tell us to forget about the earlier Commandments, but to teach us how to implement them and to do so in an easier way. We talk about things that are bad luck. It had to take my grandma to put things into perspective for me. She told me to listen that there is only one-bad luck; you miss Heaven and go to h-e-l-l. Let us not miss Heaven by doing what we want to do; that is, doing what is wrong by not obeying God's Commandments. This is why Jesus embedded in us to do what is right, and that love conquers all.

Just to ensure, we are all still on the same page; for those thinking that the Ten Commandments or some of them, are obsolete since they were only mentioned in the Old Testament may want to think again. Contrary to the belief, the Old and New Testaments have both mentioned each of the Ten Commandments. You can see that I referenced in each chapter the verses from the New Testament when relating to the Commandments in this book. It was to emphasize that, yes, the Ten Commandments exist throughout the Bible not just in the Old Testament. Once more, Jesus did not come to do away with the previous Commandments, but to be in accordance with them. *"Think not that I am come to destroy the law, or the prophets: I am not come to destroy, but to fulfil" (Matthew 5:17).* Technically, if we are obeying the two Commandments that Jesus spoke of we are in reality obeying all the Ten Commandments that were handed down in the Old Testament. Jesus came to show us how to be all about God, all about our Father's business. Let me go ahead and explain it a little bit more for you in the next few paragraphs.

The first four of the Commandments that Moses made aware to the Israelites were those Commandments that pertained and focused on loving God with all of what is within us. If we love God with all our heart, soul, and mind, we will not have any other gods before Him. No, there would be no idolizing, nor would we disrespect His name, and we would definitely always keep the Sabbath day holy in honoring the one and only God that created and blesses us.

Now the last six of the Commandments that Moses requested of the Israelites to obey actually pertained to loving each other. Here is a quick rundown. If we love others as ourselves, we would first start by respecting our parents, not killing anyone, we would certainly not cheat on our spouse, nor take anything that does not belong to us, nor lie on each other, and would not envy and hate on anyone or their belongings. We would be an encouragement to each other. We would show love for one another as God has shown His love towards us.

On the other hand, I do not think some people know what they are implying when they state that the Ten Commandments do not exist anymore. Therefore, by believing this, it is indicating that we can have many gods as we wish and bow down to graven images. We can swear in God's name. We can work for the whole week with no day of rest. Can I go ahead and continue? We do not have to respect our parents. We can kill whomever we want. We can cheat on our spouse. We can take other people possessions. We tell lies on everyone. We can desire what others have. So, we can do whatever evilness we want and do not have to repent for any of it.

With a capital "N-O," we do not get to choose which God's Commandments and agreements are nonexistent nor which one of them we want to obey. I can see more clearly now why there is so much immorality. Why "right" is now a "wrong" and "wrong" is a "double right." Please tell me this is not some people intellect. If so, let me go ahead and further rationale with them. Wow! I guess they also think that there are now no more rules or regulations to follow. We can now do what we like as long as we love doing, regardless of who it may hurt.

You do not have to get caught in being bogged down with all the symmetries. If you still do not completely understand, please feel free to go back and read over some other chapters in this book. It is definitely no additional charge to you. It's on the house (LOL!). In addition, go ahead and memorize for yourself at least one Bible verse that you can use as firepower to use against the devil when you are attacked. It does not have to be a long or complex one as long as it comes from the Bible. Once you use God's powerful Words, you will see how quickly your enemies will run from you and will see the greatness of God's work.

You Want to Stop Sinning...Stop

Now that you know the truth, we need to stop deliberately sinning and rejecting the sacrifice of Jesus. If we truly know the full truth about the Gospel of Jesus Christ we should not be trying to disavow what He has done. We are now no longer considered blind because we know the truth. We know that Jesus died for our sins. We know to do what is right. I am hoping that you are still not deciding to do what is wrong and that you will not continuously keep sinning. God will not be made out of a joke. There will be h-e-l-l to pay with your life. You definitely do not want to go there.

When I start thinking about the things in my life that I have written about in my books or be willing to write about; I do not mind being a witness to help anyone from perishing. No, it is not about putting my business out there in the street but it is all about God's business. My goal is to help save souls. It is all for the good of God's operation and to faithfully run His establishment.

There are three key points to reflect on sinning. The first two comes from the Book of Hebrews. The first one is regarding sinning intentionally after we have received the knowledge of Jesus dying for our sins. There remains no more sacrifice for our sins. The second one is if we reject the laws that Moses told the Israelites we will then die without mercy and our punishment will be more painful. The third point is in the first Book of Corinthians. God is always there for us and will not let us be tempted beyond our limitations, and without giving us a way out.

With all of that being mentioned above, it is important that we stop all the wickedness that is happening in our cities. Our cities should be holy and guiltless from evilness because we do not want God to turn away His covering from us. We forget too easily the way God use to persecute immediately for being disobedient. Since the punishment is not as swift as before for not following His Commandments; which is due to the persecution of Jesus

Christ's shed blood on the cross for our sins, we want to do whatever and whenever we want to do.

We have to remember that the game has not changed. We still need to obey God's Commandments. Jesus even helped us to understand them better by simplifying them for us into two Laws. Neither one of the laws have changed. There is still a curse on us if we do not comply with His Commandments. The reason why some of the things have happened in our lives has been because we have caused ourselves by being selfish and disobedient to God's Laws.

I, myself, knew that deep down inside I needed to have a closer relationship with God. What I had to do was to start putting God first in everything that I do. *"But seek ye first the kingdom of God, and his righteousness; and all these things shall be added unto you"* (Matthew 6:33). That's why I also decided to make some sacrifices to God and to give up a few things. I said I would do these things for a short period of time. I was determined not to worry about anything else, but putting God first. Once God knows He goes before all others, just watch and see how God works in everything that you do.

Just as Abraham was willing to sacrifice his son to God, he obeyed God's exact instructions. In the last step in the process Abraham did not have to sacrifice his son, but a ram was given to him instead. God knew Abraham was willing to make a true sacrifice by giving up who he loved the most. This is what I wanted to be able to do; to show God I was committed in giving Him a genuine sacrifice. I wanted to be real and give God something of importance. I did not want to continue just giving God my leftovers.

How many of us so often give our dogs our leftovers? On the other hand, should I say our scrapings? Therefore, why is God getting our scrapings too? God is entitled to so much more and then some. We need to get into a deeper and deeper personal relationship with God

89

and not just give Him what is left over. Each day that we wake up, we should try to reach to another level with God. We should be more involved in trying to do what God wants us to do and then get in line with His plan for us. If we do not set an example now, our next generation will know less and less about God, be more corrupt, and be worse off than we are. Then this will go on to the next generation.

We have to repent, make a U-turn, and fly right according to God's standards, not our standards. This will help the next generation from being as afflicted because of all the wickedness our ancestors had done, what we have done combined with their own wickedness. They would have triple trouble. They are leaning toward being more corrupt by following after and giving into other gods, such as: money, cars, clothes, cell phones, computers, sex, etc. more than being all about Almighty God. Don't be afraid to be the odd ball sometimes just because of doing what is right. We have to stop and listen to what God is trying to tell us because God's spirit is within us.

After I had began making sacrifices to God, I realized that the majority of my sacrifices were working hand in hand with God's Commandments and agreements. Yes, this is what I was supposed to have been doing anyway. It also showed me that if I obeyed His Words, He would make my sacrifices appear to be a simple process. Since I had started making sacrifices rather than giving God my leftovers, I began to mesmerize myself on what I really can do, or do without.

The more sacrifices that I made became more of an accomplishment for me because I knew that I was trying to be pleasing to God. Our bodies are a living sacrifice to God. That's why we should always want to be pleasing to God. In addition, by making these sacrifices it was a way that I could show God how appreciative I was for all that He had done for me. I was giving God all the praise. I

90

knew back in my mind that the sacrifices could be accomplished as long as I kept my faith, being true and real to God. God has been faithful to us all, but we have not been faithful to Him.

We should show our love for God by showing Him that we can do and abstain from many things by putting Him first in our lives. God gave us His best, which was His son. We need to give Him our best. We have to give our full whole heart to God by being a true worker and a forever witness for Him. We cannot forget all that God has done for us. That in itself should be reason enough for us to stop sinning and give Him all the praise and worship He deserves. He has brought us through the thick and thin.

If we just stop sinning willfully, we cannot even imagine how much God is waiting to give us. If we continue not obeying God's Commandments and not worship Him only, God will let us be a prime example of what happens when we are disobedient. Please do not let the Commandments be just empty words. Yes, we all have gone against God's Commandments at some point of time or another. God can help us to stop this continuing cycle of sin. We have to do our part and have the desire to quit just as if we had the desire to do it. We also cannot get so holy and think that the devil can't trip us up, as my son use to say. He will do all he can to catch us sleeping. We have to ask God for guidance and wisdom. He will direct us in which way we should go and how to avoid temptations. We have to encourage others to do what's right, and it starts first by loving each other to the fullest. We have to stop giving each other excuses as to why it is impossible to stop sinning. We just need to go ahead and start obeying His Commandments.

Remember that God has His angels watching over us, and His spirit is within us. God is loyal to us, and He will keep us from evil. We have to do our part and put Him first. If we follow God's Commandments our days on earth will increase and He will give us peace right here on earth. Do we not want to have peace from our enemies? Just remember, we can do "A-L-L" things with God's help. The decision we make is still up to us whether we will obey or not obey God's Commandments and agreements. We need to think wisely before we make that selection because both of the excursions are free of charge. We will just end up in different places. How will your journey be? Will your last stop be a one-way ticket to h-e-l-l or Heaven?